Xilinx® Laboratory Manual

to accompany

Cook's *Digital Electronics with PLD Integration*

Patrick Kane
Xilinx, Incorporated

Prentice
Hall

Upper Saddle River, New Jersey
Columbus, Ohio

Editor in Chief: Stephen Helba
Acquisitions Editor: Scott J. Sambucci
Production Editor: Rex Davidson
Design Coordinator: Robin G. Chukes
Cover Designer: Thomas Borah
Production Manager: Pat Tonneman

The book was printed and bound by Victor Graphics, Inc.
The cover was printed by Victor Graphics, Inc.

Xilinx is a registered trademark of Xilinx, Incorporated.

10 9 8 7 6 5 4 3 2 1

ISBN 0-13-088888-5

CONTENTS

Experiment 1 Quick Start Lab

Introduction

The purpose of this lab is to demonstrate a complete design starting from a "clean sheet." The design is intended to be extremely simple.

Objectives

After completing this lab, students will be able to:
- Create a completely new design from a "clean sheet," start to download.
- Understand the basic design flow, as composed of Design Entry, Design Implementation, and in-system verification.

Preliminary Procedure
1) Connect one end of the parallel cable to the parallel port of the computer. Connect the other end of the cable to the Digilab SpartanXL board as shown in the picture.

Figure 1

2) Plug the power supply into the Digilab SpartanXL board.

3) Turn on the computer.

4) After the computer is booted up, you are ready to proceed.

Procedure

Creating a New Design with the Xilinx Foundation Series Schematic

1) Start Foundation Series: **Start → Programs → Xilinx Foundation Series → Xilinx Foundation Project Manager**.

2) In the **Name** edit box; type "**OR_gate**", since this will be your design.

3) Under **Directory**, type in or Browse... to "**C:\F21_LABS**" (or the directory your lab instructor indicates).

4) As necessary, change **Family**, **Part**, and **Speed** to **"SPARTANXL"**, **"XSC10XL-PC84C"**, and **"3"**, respectively. Click **<OK>.**

5) A new project is created for you. Click on the **AND gate** icon in the Design Entry box on the right side of the Project Manager screen. The Schematic Editor will appear with a blank sheet.

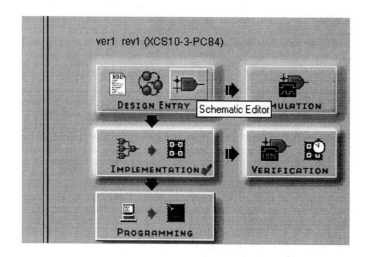

Creating a New Schematic Design in Foundation Express

You want to create a design that looks like Figure 2:

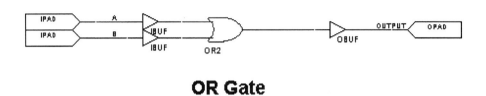

OR Gate

Figure 2

6) First, <u>click</u> on the **Symbols Toolbox** icon ![icon]. A window appears containing hundreds of symbols to choose from.

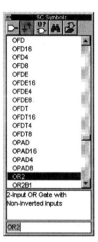

7) Type **OR2**. This is a 2-input OR-gate device. Highlight the correct macro, and then move your cursor onto the clean sheet, and <u>click</u> once to place the OR2 macro. Use the "Esc" key to get out of the macro placement mode.

8) Now you can start adding the other symbols – **IPAD, IBUF, OBUF, OPAD**.

9) Once you have added and positioned the various symbols, <u>click</u> again on the Symbols Toolbox icon, and the SC Symbols box will disappear.

10) Add wires, or nets, by <u>clicking</u> on the **Draw Wires** ![icon] icon.

11) Label wires by <u>double-clicking</u> on the nets as shown in the schematic diagram above. <u>Label</u> macros by <u>double-clicking</u> on them and renaming the existing computer-generated reference entries.

12) <u>Add</u> pin locations as **attributes** to the I/O pads. Do this by <u>double-clicking</u> each input and output pad, so that the Symbol Properties dialog box appears. Start with the input pad labeled **A1** as shown in the schematic in Figure 1. In the **Name** box, <u>type</u> "**LOC**", for pin location. In the **Description** box, type the appropriate pin number. For **A1**, using the Digilab SpartanXL™ board, it is "**P28**". <u>Click</u> on **Add** to add this attribute. Then <u>double-click</u> this entry twice (if necessary)so that two asterisks (**) appear by "LOC=P28", as in the diagram below. This will make the full attribute text visible. <u>Click</u> **Apply**, then **Move**. This will apply the attribute and allow you to move the text to a comfortable location near the IO pad.

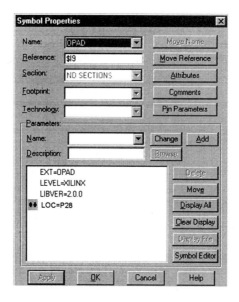

13) Once you finish creating the desired schematic, make sure to save it. <u>Click</u> **File → Save**. Then return to the Foundation Project Manager (Press **<Alt> + <Tab>** to task switch.)

14) The design entry is finished. Notice that "**or_gate1.SCH**" has been added to the **or_gate** Project Description File (**PDF**).

15) Now we must implement this design. <u>Click</u> on the **Implementation icon.** <u>Select</u> "Yes" to update the netlist based on the last saved design. The software converts Foundation Schematic files into an EDIF (Electronic Data Interchange Format), netlist and opens up the **Xilinx Flow Manager**.

16) Project **or_gate** is highlighted. <u>Select</u> **Design → Implement...** Make sure that the part selected is "XCS10XL-PC84" (if using the Spartan board). Note also that this will be version '**ver1**' and revision '**rev1**'. <u>Click</u> **Run**.

17) When the flow engine has finished placing and routing your design, a dialog box will appear to indicate successful completion. Click on "OK" in the dialog box.

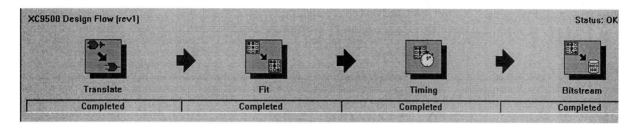

Flow Engine

Downloading and Testing Your Design

18) FPGAs require that you download a BIT file (.bit extension) program. With the **Digilab SpartanXL board**, this download is done via a basic parallel cable and the **Xilinx Programming** utility download software included in the Foundation package. This software should already be loaded on your computer.

    a) Click on the PROGRAMMING icon.

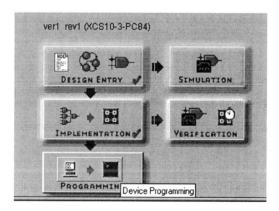

    b) Select Hardware Debugger and the "OK".
    c) Click on "Output" and select "Cable Auto connect" from the pull-down menu.
    d) Click on File>Open.

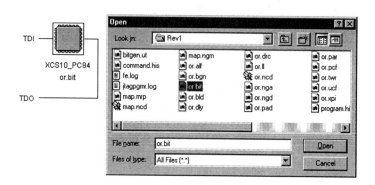

e) Select "or.bit" and click on Open.

f) On the main menu bar select Operations>Program and the .bit file will be loaded into the device and the device will be configured.

Congratulations! You have created and implemented a new project on your own.

Activity Sheet Experiment 1
Quick Start OR-Gate Lab

Name: _____

Date: _____

Step 1: Connect an oscilloscope or multimeter to the output pin. You can see which post to connect this to by examining the mapping diagram for the XS95 and Xstend boards.

Step 2: Using the switches on the board, set them to each of the input conditions in Table 1-1 and record the output, as measured by the multimeter or oscilloscope, as a logical 1 (>2 VDC) or a logical 0 (<2 VDC) or observe the LEDs.

Input A	Input B	Output
0	0	
1	0	
0	1	
1	1	

Step 3: In your own words describe and explain the results shown in Table 1-1.

_____

_____

_____

_____

_____

Step 4: Give a brief explanation of how the circuit works explaining why the circuit reacts the way it does to each of the different input combinations.

_____

_____

_____

_____

_____

Experiment 2 Inverter Lab

Introduction

The purpose of this lab is to build and download an inverter using the Xilinx Foundation tools and Digilab SpartanXL board.

Objectives

After completing this lab, students will be able to:
- Demonstrate the truth-table operation of an inverter.
- Perform a simple functional simulation using the integrated simulation tool.

Preliminary Procedure

Follow the same steps as in the "Quick Start OR-Gate lab" to set up the lab board.

Procedure

Follow the same steps as in the OR-Gate lab to create a new design with the Xilinx Foundation Series Schematic except in this case name the design Inverter. Consult the pin table for the specific board you are using to determine where to lock the input and output pins.

Creating a New Schematic Design in Foundation Express

You want to create a design that looks like Figure 1:

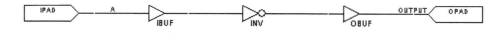

Inverter

Figure 1

1) First, <u>click</u> on the **Symbols Toolbox** icon 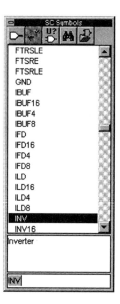. A window appears containing hundreds of symbols to choose from.

2) Type **INV**. This is an inverter. Highlight the correct macro, and then move your cursor onto the clean sheet, and <u>click</u> once to place the Inverter macro. Use the "Esc" key to get out of macro placement mode.

3) Now you can start adding the other symbols – **IPAD, IBUF, OBUF,** and **OPAD**.

4) Once you have added and positioned the various symbols, <u>click</u> again on the Symbols Toolbox icon, and the SC Symbols box will disappear.

5) <u>Add</u> wires and label them as in the "Quick Start OR-Gate lab."

6) <u>Add</u> pin locations as in the "Quick Start OR-Gate lab."

7) Once you finish creating the desired schematic, make sure to save it. <u>Click</u> **File → Save**. Then return to the Foundation Project Manager (press **<Alt>** + **<Tab>** to task switch).

8) The design entry is finished. Notice that "`inverter1.SCH`" has been added to the `inverter` Project Description File (**PDF**).

Activity Sheet Experiment 2
Inverter (NOT) Function

Name: _____

Date: _____

Using the Simulator

Step 1:
To simulate the operation of the inverter, first click on the SIM icon in the menu bar at the top of the schematic screen. The Logic Simulator will open.

Step 2:
Next, click on Signal -> Add Signals in the menu bar at the top of the simulator screen. Here you can decide which signals to drive and observe during the simulation. Note that the signals available are A, Output (from the schematic), and something called SimGlobalReset. What SimGlobalReset does is to simulate a global reset on the PLD. It is always a good idea to use this initially just to ensure that you have a totally reset simulation before you start to drive signals.
Double-click on all three signals (there will be a red checkmark to indicate selection). Then click on CLOSE at the bottom of the screen.

Step 3:
Now click on Signals -> Add Stimulators in the menu bar at the top of the simulator screen. A box that looks like a keyboard will open. Click on the signal "A" in the upper-left portion of the screen and then on the "A" on the keyboard (on the screen). Click on "SimGlobalReset" and then on the keyboard click on "R". We can now drive the "A" input and the global reset. Pressing the "R" key will toggle the reset and pressing the "A" key will toggle the input to the inverter.

Step 4:
Toggle both the "R" and the "A" keys (toggle "A" until it is a logical one) and then click on the "footsteps" in the menu bar at the top of the screen. If "A" is a logical "1" then "Output" is a logical _____. Toggle "A" now "Output" is a logical _____.

Step 5:
To perform a timing simulation, simply change the pull-down menu in the menu bar of the simulator screen from "Functional" to "Timing" and you will get the actual post route timing.

NOTE: You will need to perform timing simulation in some of the later labs because functional simulation will cause glitching in some types of circuits. This will be explained fully in those labs.

Step 6:
Now we must implement this design as in the "Quick Start OR-Gate lab."

Downloading and Testing Your Design

Step 7:
The next step is to download the design to the Digilab SpartanXL board as in the "Quick Start OR-gate lab."

Step 8:
Connect an oscilloscope or multimeter to the output pin. You can see which post to connect this to by examining the mapping diagram for the Digilab SpartanXL board.

Step 9:
Using the switches on the Digilab board, set it to the two input conditions in Table 2-1 and record the output, as measured by the multimeter or oscilloscope, as a logical 1 (>2 VDC) or a logical 0 (<2 VDC); or observe the leftmost LED.

Input A	Output
0	
1	

Table 2-1

Step 10:
In your own words describe and explain the results shown in Table 2-1.

_____

_____

_____

_____

_____

Step 11:
Give a brief explanation of how the circuit works explaining why the circuit reacts the way it does to each of the different inputs.

_____

_____

_____

_____

_____

Experiment 3 AND-Gate Lab

Introduction

The purpose of this lab is to build and download a three-input AND gate using the Xilinx Foundation tools Digilab SpartanXL board.

Objectives

After completing this lab, students will be able to:
- Demonstrate the truth-table operation of an AND gate.

Preliminary Procedure

Follow the same steps as in the "Quick Start OR-Gate lab" to set up the lab board.

Procedure

Follow the same steps as in the OR-Gate lab to create a new design with the Xilinx Foundation Series Schematic except in this case name the design AND_gate. Consult the pin table for the specific board you are using to determine where to lock the input and output pins.

Creating a New Schematic Design in Foundation Express

You want to create a design that looks like this:

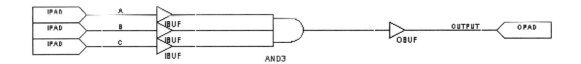

AND Gate

Figure 1

1) First, click on the **Symbols Toolbox** icon 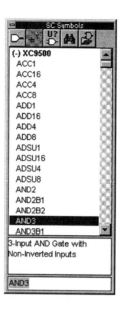. A window appears containing hundreds of symbols to choose from.

2) Type **AND3**. This is a 3-input AND gate device. Highlight the correct macro, and then move your cursor onto the clean sheet, and click once to place the AND3 macro. Use the "Esc" key to get out of macro placement mode.

3) Now you can start adding the other symbols – **IPAD, IBUF, OBUF,** and **OPAD.**

4) Once you have added and positioned the various symbols, click again on the Symbols Toolbox icon, and the SC Symbols box will disappear.

5) Add wires and label them as in the "Quick Start OR-Gate lab."

6) Add pin locations as in the "Quick Start OR-Gate lab."

7) Once you finish creating the desired schematic, make sure to save it. Click **File → Save**. Then return to the Foundation Project Manager (press **<Alt> + <Tab>** to task switch).

8) The design entry is finished. Notice that "**AND_gate1.SCH**" has been added to the **AND-gate** Project Description File (**PDF**).

9) Now we must implement this design as in the "Quick Start OR-Gate lab."

Activity Sheet Experiment 3
AND-Gate Lab

Name: _____

Date: _____

Downloading and Testing Your Design

Step 1:
The next step is to download the design to the Digilab board as described in the Quick Start lab.

Step 2:
To test the AND gate design, use the switches on the board and observe the LEDs.

Step 3:
Connect an oscilloscope or multimeter to the output pin. You can see which post to connect this to by examining the mapping diagram for the Digilab board.

Step 4:
Using the switches on the Digilab board, set them to each of the input conditions in Table 3-1 and record the output, as measured by the multimeter or oscilloscope, as a logical 1 (>2 VDC) or a logical 0 (<2 VDC).

Input A	Input B	Output
0	0	
1	0	
0	1	
1	1	

Table 3-1

Step 5:
In your own words describe and explain the results shown in Table 3-1.

_____

_____

_____

_____

Step 6:
Give a brief explanation of how the circuit works explaining why the circuit reacts the way it does to each of the different input combinations.

_____

_____

_____

_____

_____

Experiment 4 NOR-Gate Lab

Introduction

The purpose of this lab is to build and download a NOR gate using the Xilinx Foundation tools and Digilab SpartanXL board.

Objectives

After completing this lab, students will be able to:
- Demonstrate the truth-table operation of a NAND gate.

Preliminary Procedure

Follow the same steps as in the "Clean Start OR-Gate lab" to set up the lab board.

Procedure

Follow the same steps as in the OR-Gate lab to create a new design with the Xilinx Foundation Series Schematic except in this case name the design NAND. Consult the pin table for the specific board you are using to determine where to lock the input and output pins.

Creating a New Schematic Design in Foundation Express

You want to create a design that looks like this:

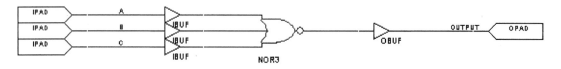

NOR Gate

Figure 1

1) First, <u>click</u> on the **Symbols Toolbox** icon 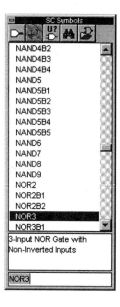. A window appears containing hundreds of symbols to choose from.

2) Type **NOR3**. This is a 3-input NOR gate. Highlight the correct macro, and then move your cursor onto the clean sheet, and <u>click</u> once to place the NOR3 macro. Use the "Esc" key to get out of macro placement mode.

3) Now you can start adding the other symbols – **IPAD, IBUF, OBUF,** and **OPAD**.

4) Once you have added and positioned the various symbols, <u>click</u> again on the Symbols Toolbox icon, and the SC Symbols box will disappear.

5) Add wires and label them as in the "Clean Start OR-Gate lab."

6) <u>Add</u> pin locations as in the "Clean Start OR-Gate lab."

7) Once you finish creating the desired schematic, make sure to save it. <u>Click</u> **File → Save**. Then return to the Foundation Project Manager (press **<Alt>** + **<Tab>** to task switch).

8) The design entry is finished. Notice that "**NOR1.SCH**" has been added to the **nor** Project Description File (**PDF**).

9) Now we must implement this design as in the "Clean Start OR-Gate lab."

Activity Sheet Experiment 4
NOR-Gate Lab

Name: _____

Date: _____

Downloading and Testing Your Design

Step 1:
Download the design to the board as in the "Clean Start OR-Gate lab."

Step 2:
To test the NOR design use the switches on the board and observe the LED.

Step 3:
Derive the truth table of the 3-input NOR gate either by using the simulator as described in the inverter lab or by using the output at the LED.
Connect an oscilloscope or multimeter to the output pin. You can see which post to connect this to by examining the mapping diagram for the Digilab board.

Step 4:
Using the switches on the Digilab board, set them to each of the input conditions in Table 4-1 and record the output, as measured by the multimeter or oscilloscope, as a logical 1 (>2 VDC) or a logical 0 (<2 VDC).

Input A	Input B	Output
0	0	
1	0	
0	1	
1	1	

Table 4-1

Step 5:
In your own words describe and explain the results shown in Table 4-1.

_____

_____

_____

_____

_____

Step 6:
Give a brief explanation of how the circuit works explaining why the circuit reacts the way it does to each of the different input combinations.

_____

_____

_____

_____

_____

Experiment 5 NAND-Gate Lab

Introduction

The purpose of this lab is to build and download a NAND gate using the Xilinx Foundation tools and Digilab SpartanXL board.

Objective

After completing this lab, students will be able to:
- Demonstrate the truth-table operation of a NAND gate.

Preliminary Procedure

Follow the same steps as in the "Quick Start OR-Gate lab" to set up the lab board.

Procedure

Follow the same steps as in the OR-Gate lab to create a new design with Xilinx Foundation Series Schematic except in this case name the design NAND. Consult the pin table for the specific board you are using to determine where to lock the input and output pins.

You want to create a design that looks like this:

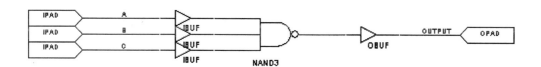

NAND Gate

Figure 1

1) First, <u>click</u> on the **Symbols Toolbox** icon 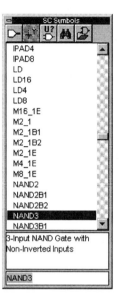. A window appears containing hundreds of symbols to choose from.

2) Type **NAND3**. This is a 3-input NAND gate. Highlight the correct macro, and then move your cursor onto the clean sheet, and <u>click</u> once to place the NAND3 macro. Use the "Esc" key to get out of macro placement mode.

3) Now you can start adding the other symbols – **IPAD, IBUF, OBUF,** and **OPAD**.

4) Once you have added and positioned the various symbols, <u>click</u> again on the Symbols Toolbox icon, and the SC Symbols box will disappear.

5) <u>Add</u> wires and label them as in the "Quick Start OR-Gate lab."

6) <u>Add</u> pin locations as in the "Quick Start OR-Gate lab."

7) Once you finish creating the desired schematic, make sure to save it. <u>Click</u> **File → Save**. Then return to the Foundation Project Manager (press **<Alt> + <Tab>** to task switch).

8) The design entry is finished. Notice that "**NAND1.SCH**" has been added to the **NAND** Project Description File (**PDF**).

9) Now we must implement this design as in the "Quick Start OR-Gate lab."

Activity Sheet Experiment 5
NAND-Gate Lab

Name: _____

Date: _____

Downloading and Testing Your Design

Step 1:
Download the design to the board as in the "Clean Start OR-Gate lab."

Step 2:
To test the NOR design, use the switches on the Digilab board and observe the LED.

Step 3:
Derive the truth table of the NAND gate either by using the simulator as described in the inverter lab or by using the output at the LED.
Connect an oscilloscope or multimeter to the output pin. You can see which post to connect this to by examining the pin mapping diagram for the board.

Step 4:
Using the switches on the board, set them to each of the input conditions in Table 5-1 and record the output, as measured by the multimeter or oscilloscope, as a logical 1 (>2 VDC) or a logical 0 (<2 VDC).

Input A	Input B	Output
0	0	
1	0	
0	1	
1	1	

Table 5-1

Step 5:
In your own words describe and explain the results shown in Table 5-1.

_____

_____

_____

_____

Step 6:
Give a brief explanation of how the circuit works explaining why the circuit reacts the way it does to each of the different input combinations.

_____

_____

_____

_____

_____

Experiment 6 XOR-Gate Lab

Introduction

The purpose of this lab is to build and download an XOR gate using the Xilinx Foundation tools and Digilab SpartanXL board.

Objectives

After completing this lab, students will be able to:
- Demonstrate the truth-table operation of an XOR gate.

Preliminary Procedure

Follow the same steps as in the "Quick Start OR-Gate lab" to set up the lab board.

Procedure

Follow the same steps as in the OR-Gate lab to create a new design with the Xilinx Foundation Series Schematic except in this case name the design XOR. Consult the pin table for the specific board you are using to determine where to lock the input and output pins.

You want to create a design that looks like this:

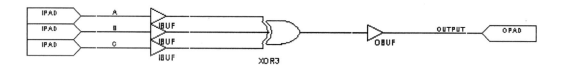

XOR Gate

Figure 1

1) First, click on the **Symbols Toolbox** icon 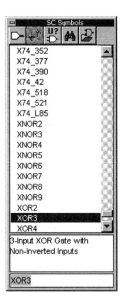. A window appears containing hundreds of symbols to choose from.

2) Type **XOR3**. This is a 3-input XOR gate. Highlight the correct macro, and then move your cursor onto the clean sheet, and click once to place the XOR3 macro. Use the "Esc" key to get out of macro placement mode.

3) Now you can start adding the other symbols – **IPAD, IBUF, OBUF,** and **OPAD**.

4) Once you have added and positioned the various symbols, click again on the Symbols Toolbox icon, and the SC Symbols box will disappear.

5) Add wires and label them as in the "Quick Start OR-Gate lab."

6) Add pin locations as in the "Quick Start OR-Gate lab."

7) Once you finish creating the desired schematic, make sure to save it. Click **File → Save**. Then return to the Foundation Project Manager (press **<Alt> + <Tab>** to task switch).

8) The design entry is finished. Notice that "**XOR1.SCH**" has been added to the **XOR** Project Description File (**PDF**).

9) Now we must implement this design as in the "Quick Start OR-Gate lab."

Activity Sheet Experiment 6
XOR-Gate Lab

Name: _____

Date: _____

Downloading and Testing Your Design

Step 1: Download the design to the board as in the "Clean Start OR-gate lab."

Step 2: To test the XOR design, use the switches on the Digilab board and observe the LED.

Step 3: Derive the truth table of the XOR gate either by using the simulator as described in the inverter lab or by using the output at the LED.
Connect an oscilloscope or multimeter to the output pin. You can see which post to connect this to by examining the mapping diagram for the board.

Step 4: Using the switches on the board, set them to each of the input conditions in Table 6-1 and record the output, as measured by the multimeter or oscilloscope, as a logical 1 (>2 VDC) or a logical 0 (<2 VDC).

Input A	Input B	Output
0	0	
1	0	
0	1	
1	1	

Table 6-1

Step 5: In your own words describe and explain the results shown in Table 6-1.

_____

_____

_____

_____

_____

Step 6: Give a brief explanation of how the circuit works explaining why the circuit reacts the way it does to each of the different input combinations.

_____

_____

_____

_____

_____

Experiment 7 XNOR-Gate Lab

Introduction

The purpose of this lab is to build and download an XNOR gate using the Xilinx Foundation tools and Digilab SpartanXL board.

Objectives

After completing this lab, students will be able to:

- Demonstrate the truth-table operation of an XNOR gate.

Preliminary Procedure

Follow the same steps as in the "Quick Start OR-Gate lab" to set up the lab board.

Procedure

Follow the same steps as in the OR-Gate lab to create a new design project with the Xilinx Foundation Series Schematic except in this case name the design XNOR. Consult the pin table for the specific board you are using to determine where to lock the input and output pins.

You want to create a design that looks like this:

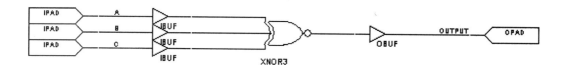

XNOR Gate

Figure 1

1) First, click on the **Symbols Toolbox** icon . A window appears containing hundreds of symbols to choose from.

2) Type **XNOR3**. This is a 3-input XNOR gate. Highlight the correct macro, and then move your cursor onto the clean sheet, and click once to place the XNOR3 macro. Use the "Esc" key to get out of macro placement mode.

3) Now you can start adding the other symbols – **IPAD, IBUF, OBUF,** and **OPAD**.

4) Once you have added and positioned the various symbols, click again on the Symbols Toolbox icon, and the SC Symbols box will disappear.

5) Add wires and label them as in the "Quick Start OR-Gate lab."

6) Add pin locations as in the "Quick Start OR- Gate lab."

7) Once you finish creating the desired schematic, make sure to save it. Click **File → Save**. Then return to the Foundation Project Manager (press **<Alt>** + **<Tab>** to task switch).

8) The design entry is finished. Notice that "**XNOR1.SCH**" has been added to the **XNOR** Project Description File (**PDF**).

9) Now we must implement this design as in the "Quick Start OR-Gate lab."

Activity Sheet Experiment 7
XNOR-Gate Lab

Name: _____

Date: _____

Downloading and Testing Your Design

Step 1: Download the design to the board as in the "Clean Start OR-Gate lab."

Step 2: To test the XNOR design, use the switches on the Digilab board and observe the LED.

Step 3: Derive the truth table of the XNOR gate either by using the simulator as described in the inverter lab or by using the output at the LED.
Connect an oscilloscope or multimeter to the output pin. You can see which pin to connect this to by examining the mapping diagram for the board.

Step 4: Using the switches on the board, set them to each of the input conditions in the table and record the output, as measured by the multimeter or oscilloscope, as a logical 1 (>2 VDC) or a logical 0 (<2 VDC).

Input A	Input B	Output
0	0	
1	0	
0	1	
1	1	

Step 5: In your own words describe and explain the results shown in the table.

_____

_____

_____

_____

_____

Step 6: Give a brief explanation of how the circuit works explaining why the circuit reacts
the way it does to each of the different input combinations.

_____

_____

_____

_____

_____

Experiment 8
Basic Decoders Lab

Introduction

The purpose of this lab is to build, simulate, and download two basic decoders using the Xilinx Foundation tools and Digilab SpartanXL board.

Objectives

After completing this lab, students will be able to:
- Demonstrate the truth-table operation of the two basic decoders described.
- Perform a simple functional simulation using the integrated simulation tool.

Preliminary Procedure

Follow the same steps as in the "Quick Start OR-Gate lab" to set up the lab board.

Procedure

Create a new design with the Xilinx Foundation Series Schematic and name the design Decoders. Consult the pin table for the specific board you are using to determine where to lock the input and output pins.

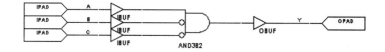

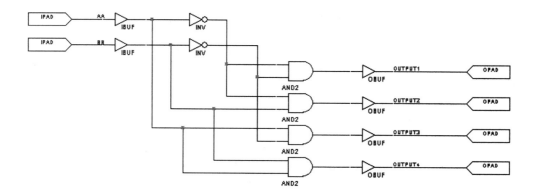

Basic Decoders

You want to create a design that looks like the schematic above.

1) Once you finish creating the desired schematic, make sure to save it. Click **File → Save**. Then return to the Foundation Project Manager (press **<Alt>** + **<Tab>** to task switch).

2) The design entry is finished.

HDL Alternative

Here is the code for the lab in VDHL. Follow the design flow in the "Using Hardware Design Languages (HDLs) with Xilinx tools" tutorial in the appendix. Don't forget to lock the pins in the ".ucf" file.

```
library IEEE;                  -- Declares the IEEE library
use IEEE.std_logic_1164.all;        -- Uses std_logic from IEEE library

entity decoders is             -- Entity declaration for design
  port (                  -- Port declarations
      A: in STD_LOGIC;
      B: in STD_LOGIC;
      C: in STD_LOGIC;
      AA: in STD_LOGIC;
      BB: in STD_LOGIC;
      Y: out STD_LOGIC;
      OUTPUT1: out STD_LOGIC;
      OUTPUT2: out STD_LOGIC;
      OUTPUT3: out STD_LOGIC;
      OUTPUT4: out STD_LOGIC
  );
end decoders;              -- End of entity declaration

architecture rtl of decoders is      -- Start of architecture declaration
begin
  Y <= (A and (not B) and (not C));   -- Several concurrent VHDL statements
  OUTPUT1 <= (not AA) and (not BB);   -- which describe the design
  OUTPUT2 <= (not AA) and BB;
  OUTPUT3 <= AA and (not BB);
  OUTPUT4 <= AA and BB;
end rtl;                  -- End of architecture declaration
```

Here is the design again in the Verilog HDL language:

```verilog
module decoders (A, B, C, AA, BB, Y, OUTPUT1, OUTPUT2, OUTPUT3, OUTPUT4);
    input A;
    input B;
    input C;
    input AA;
    input BB;
    output Y;
    output OUTPUT1;
    output OUTPUT2;
    output OUTPUT3;
    output OUTPUT4;

    reg Y;
    reg OUTPUT1;
    reg OUTPUT2;
    reg OUTPUT3;
    reg OUTPUT4;

    always @(A or B or C or AA or BB)
        begin: decode
            Y = (A & ~B & ~C);
            OUTPUT1 = ~AA & ~BB;
            OUTPUT2 = ~AA & BB;
            OUTPUT3 = AA & ~BB;
            OUTPUT4 = AA & BB;
        end
endmodule
```

Briefly describe the similarities and differences between the VHDL and Verilog versions of the design:

_____

_____

_____

_____

_____

Activity Sheet Experiment 8
Basic Decoders Lab

Name: _____

Date: _____

Using the Simulator

Step 1:
This is another chance to practice with the Aldec™ logic simulation tool integrated with the Xilinx software. To simulate the operation of the decoders first click on the SIM icon in the menu bar at the top of the schematic screen. The Logic Simulator will open.

Step 2:
Next, click on Signal -> Add Signals in the menu bar at the top of the simulator screen. Here you can decide which signals to drive and observe during the simulation. Note that the signals available are A, B, C, AA, and BB as well as the five outputs: Y and Output1 through 4 (from the schematic), and something called SimGlobalReset. Recall that what SimGlobalReset does is to simulate a global reset on the PLD. It is always a good idea to use this initially just to ensure that you have a totally reset simulation before you start to drive signals.
Double-click on all of the signals (there will be a red checkmark to indicate selection). Then click on CLOSE at the bottom of the screen.

Step 3:
Now click on Signals -> Add Stimulators in the menu bar at the top of the simulator screen. A box that looks like a keyboard will open. Click on the signal "A" in the upper-left portion of the screen and then on the "A" on the keyboard (on the screen). Do the same for B, C, AA, and BB using letters from the keyboard of your choice. Then click on "SimGlobalReset" and then on the keyboard click on "R". We can now drive the inputs and the global reset.
Pressing the "R" key will toggle the reset and pressing the "A" key will toggle the "A" input to the AND gate in the first decoder.

Step 4:
Toggle the "R" and the input signals and then click on the "footsteps" in the menu bar at the top of the screen. Complete the following truth tables:

Basic Decoder Function Tables

Ckt. (a)				Ckt. (b)						
C	B	A	Y	AA	BB	1	2	3	4
0	0	0		0	0				
0	0	1		0	1				
0	1	0		1	0				
0	1	1		1	1				
1	0	0							
1	0	1							
1	1	0							
1	1	1							

Table 8-1

Downloading and Testing Your Design

Step 5: Download the design to the board as in the "Clean Start OR-Gate lab."

Step 6:
To test the design, use switches on the board and observe the LEDs.

Step 7:
Derive the truth table of the circuits using the LEDs on the board or
connect an oscilloscope or multimeter to the output pin. You can see which post to connect
this to by examining the mapping diagram for the Digilab board.

Step 8:
Using the switches on the board, set them to each of the input conditions in Table 8-2 and
record the output, as measured by the multimeter or oscilloscope, as a logical 1 (>2 VDC) or
a logical 0 (<2 VDC). Verify that these are the same output data you got from the simulator.

Basic Decoder Function Tables

Ckt. (a)				Ckt. (b)						
C	B	A	Y	AA	BB	1	2	3	4
0	0	0		0	0				
0	0	1		0	1				
0	1	0		1	0				
0	1	1		1	1				
1	0	0							
1	0	1							
1	1	0							
1	1	1							

Table 8-2

Step 9:
In your own words describe and explain the results shown in Table 8-1.

_____

_____

_____

_____

_____

Step 10:
Give a brief explanation of how the circuit works, explaining why the circuit reacts the way it does to each of the different input combinations.

_____

_____

_____

_____

_____

Experiment 9
BCD-to-Decimal Counter Lab

Introduction

The purpose of this lab is to build and download two basic decoders using the Xilinx Foundation tools and Digilab SpartanXL board.

Objectives

After completing this lab, students will be able to:
- Build a BCD-to-decimal counter circuit.
- Verify the operation of the circuit using a simulator and a demo board.

Preliminary Procedure

Follow the same steps as in the "Quick Start OR-Gate lab" to set up the lab board.

Procedure

Create a new design with the Xilinx Foundation Series Schematic and name the design BCD2DEC. Consult the pin table for the specific board you are using to determine where to lock the input and output pins.
You want to create a design that looks like Figure 1:

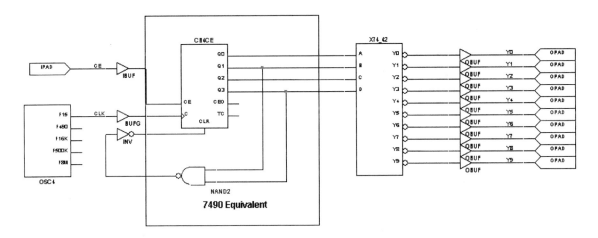

BCD-to-Decimal Counter

Figure 1

1) Once you finish creating the desired schematic, make sure to save it. Click **File** → **Save**. Then return to the Foundation Project Manager (press **<Alt>** + **<Tab>** to task switch).

2) The design entry is finished.

HDL Alternative

Here is the code for the lab in VDHL. Follow the design flow in the "Using Hardware Design Languages (HDLs) with Xilinx tools" tutorial. Don't forget to lock the pins in the ".ucf" file.

```
library IEEE;
use IEEE.std_logic_1164.all;

entity BCD2DEC is
  port (
      RST: in STD_LOGIC;
      CE: in STD_LOGIC;
    Y: out STD_LOGIC_VECTOR (7 downto 0)
  );
end BCD2DEC;

architecture rtl of BCD2DEC is
    component clock              -- Component declaration
      port (                -- Port declaration
        clk_out: inout std_logic   -- Component signals
      );
    end component;                 -- End of component declaration

    type BCD_type is (S0, S1, S2, S3, S4, S5, S6, S7);  -- User type for
    signal cs_BCD, ns_BCD: BCD_type;   -- State machine, cs: current state,
    signal clk: STD_LOGIC;           -- ns: next state, clk is our
begin                     -- internal clock
    generate_clock: clock          -- Mapping to internal clock generator
      port map (clk);

    change_out_ns: process (cs_BCD)    -- Beginning of process statement
    begin
      case cs_BCD is              -- Case statement which changes the
        when S0 =>              -- output and the next state based
          ns_BCD <= S1;          -- upon a change in the current state
            Y <= "10000000";       -- This process is triggered when, and
        when S1 =>              -- only when cs_BCD changes as stated
```

```vhdl
    ns_BCD <= S2;        -- by the process sensitivity list
        Y <= "01000000";
    when S2 =>
      ns_BCD <= S3;
        Y <= "00100000";
    when S3 =>
      ns_BCD <= S4;
        Y <= "00010000";
    when S4 =>
      ns_BCD <= S5;
        Y <= "00001000";
    when S5 =>
      ns_BCD <= S6;
      Y <= "00000100";
    when S6 =>
      ns_BCD <= S7;
      Y <= "00000010";
    when S7 =>
      ns_BCD <= S0;
      Y <= "00000001";
    when others =>
      ns_BCD <= S0;
      Y <= "10000000";
  end case;
end process change_out_ns;       -- End of process statement

change_cs: process(clk, RST, CE)  -- Process which resets the circuit
begin                  -- and assigns the current state
    if (RST='1') then        -- based upon next state
      cs_BCD <= S0;
    elsif (CE='1') then
      if rising_edge(clk) then
      cs_BCD <= ns_BCD;
    end if;
  end if;
end process change_cs;
end rtl;
```

Here is the design again in the Verilog HDL language:

```
module decoders (A, B, C, AA, BB, Y, OUTPUT1, OUTPUT2, OUTPUT3, OUTPUT4);
    input A;
    input B;
    input C;
    input AA;
    input BB;
    output Y;
    output OUTPUT1;
    output OUTPUT2;
    output OUTPUT3;
    output OUTPUT4;

    reg Y;
    reg OUTPUT1;
    reg OUTPUT2;
    reg OUTPUT3;
    reg OUTPUT4;

    always @(A or B or C or AA or BB)
        begin: decode
            Y = (A & ~B & ~C);
            OUTPUT1 = ~AA & ~BB;
            OUTPUT2 = ~AA & BB;
            OUTPUT3 = AA & ~BB;
            OUTPUT4 = AA & BB;
        end
endmodule
```

Briefly describe the similarities and differences between the VHDL and Verilog versions of the design:

_____

_____

_____

_____

_____

Activity Sheet Experiment 9
BCD-to-Decimal Counter Lab

Name: _____

Date: _____

Using the Simulator

Step1:
You will once again use the Aldec™ logic simulation tool integrated with the Xilinx software to verify the functional operation of the circuit. To simulate the operation of the counter, first click on the SIM icon in the menu bar at the top of the schematic screen. The Logic Simulator will open.

Click on Signal -> Add Signals in the menu bar at the top of the simulator screen. Here you can decide which signals to drive and observe during the simulation. Note that the signals available are CE, CLK, and Y0-Y9, as the ten outputs (from the schematic), and something called SimGlobalReset. Recall that what SimGlobalReset does is to simulate a global reset on the PLD. It is always a good idea to use this initially just to ensure that you have a totally reset simulation before you start to drive signals.

Double click on all of the signals (there will be a red checkmark to indicate selection). Then click on CLOSE at the bottom of the screen.

Step 2:
Now click on Signals -> Add Stimulators in the menu bar at the top of the simulator screen. A box that looks like a keyboard will open. Click on the signal CE in the upper-left portion of the screen and then on the "C" on the keyboard (on the screen). Then click on "SimGlobalReset" and then on the keyboard click on "R". Next click on "CLK" and then go over to the keyboard screen and click on the oval just beneath the "0" on the line labeled Bc:. This is how you can select a clock using the simulator. Other ovals in that group define certain characteristics of clocks such as Non-Return to Zero (NRZ). If you are interested in learning more about this topic just click on "Help" and then "Using Simulator".

You can now drive the inputs and the global reset. Pressing the "R" key will toggle the reset and pressing the "C" key will toggle the Clock Enable "CE" input to the Decade Counter.

Step 3:
Toggle the "R" and "CE" signals and then click on the "footsteps" in the menu bar at the top of the screen. Complete the following truth table:

BCD-to-Decimal Function Table					
	BCD Input				Decimal Output
No.	D	C	B	A	0 1 2 3 4 5 6 7 8 9
0	L	L	L	L	
1	L	L	L	H	
2	L	L	H	L	
3	L	L	H	H	
4	L	H	L	L	
5	L	H	L	H	
6	L	H	H	L	
7	L	H	H	H	
8	H	L	L	L	
9	H	L	L	H	
X	H	L	H	L	X X X X X X X X X X
X	H	L	H	H	X X X X X X X X X X
X	H	H	L	L	X X X X X X X X X X
X	H	H	L	H	X X X X X X X X X X
X	H	H	H	L	X X X X X X X X X X
X	H	H	H	H	X X X X X X X X X X

Table 9-1

Step 4:
Now you can physically verify this design and truth table by implementing it as in the "Quick Start OR-Gate lab."

Downloading and Testing Your Design

Step 5:
The next step is to download the design to board as in the "Quick Start OR-Gate lab."

Step 6:
To test the decoders design, use the switches on the board and observe the LEDs. Refer to your lab book to verify which pins are connected to the switches and LEDs. Alternatively connect an oscilloscope or multimeter to the output pins. You can see which pin to connect this to by examining the pin mapping diagram for the boards.

Step 7:
Using the switches on the board, toggle the CE signal to high and then record the outputs in Table 9-2, as measured by the multimeter or oscilloscope, as a logical 1 (>2 VDC) or a logical 0 (<2 VDC).

BCD-to-Decimal Function Table														
	BCD Input				Decimal Output									
No.	D	C	B	A	0	1	2	3	4	5	6	7	8	9
0	L	L	L	L										
1	L	L	L	H										
2	L	L	H	L										
3	L	L	H	H										
4	L	H	L	L										
5	L	H	L	H										
6	L	H	H	L										
7	L	H	H	H										
8	H	L	L	L										
9	H	L	L	H										
X	H	L	H	L	X	X	X	X	X	X	X	X	X	X
X	H	L	H	H	X	X	X	X	X	X	X	X	X	X
X	H	H	L	L	X	X	X	X	X	X	X	X	X	X
X	H	H	L	H	X	X	X	X	X	X	X	X	X	X
X	H	H	H	L	X	X	X	X	X	X	X	X	X	X
X	H	H	H	H	X	X	X	X	X	X	X	X	X	X

Table 9-2

Step 8:

In your own words describe and explain the results shown in Table 9-2.

_____

_____

_____

_____

_____

Step 9:

Give a brief explanation of how the circuit works explaining why the circuit reacts the way it does to each of the different input combinations.

_____

_____

_____

_____

_____

Experiment 10 Flasher Circuit Lab

Introduction

The purpose of this lab is to build, simulate and download a 16 back-and-forth flasher circuit using the Xilinx Foundation tools and Digilab SpartanXL board.

Objectives

After completing this lab, students will be able to:
- Demonstrate the truth-table operation of an up/down counter.
- Perform a functional simulation of the flasher circuit using the integrated simulation tool.

Preliminary Procedure

Follow the same steps as in the "Quick Start OR-Gate lab" to set up the lab board.

Procedure

Create a new design with the Xilinx Foundation Series Schematic and name the design Flasher. Consult the pin table for the specific board you are using to determine where to lock the input and output pins.
You want to create a design that looks like this:

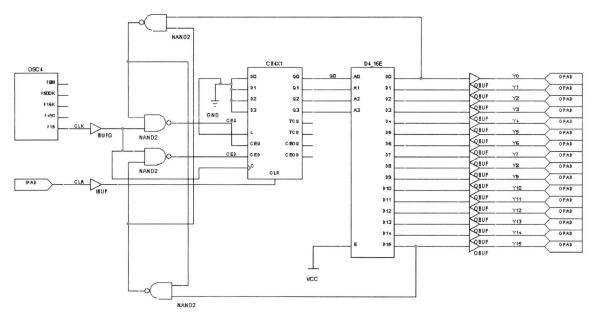

Flasher Circuit

1) Once you finish creating the desired schematic, make sure to save it. <u>Click</u> **File → Save**. Then return to the Foundation Project Manager (press **\<Alt\>** + **\<Tab\>** to task switch).

2) The design entry is finished.

Activity Sheet Experiment 10
Back-and-Forth Flasher Circuit Lab

Name: _____

Date: _____

Using the Simulator

Step 1:
This is another chance to practice with the Aldec™ logic simulation tool integrated with the Xilinx software. To simulate the operation of the decoders, first click on the SIM icon in the menu bar at the top of the schematic screen. The Logic Simulator will open.
Click on Signal -> Add Signals in the menu bar at the top of the simulator screen. Here you can decide which signals to drive and observe during the simulation. Note that the signals available are only CLK and CLR, as well as the 16 outputs: Y0-Y15, (from the schematic) and something called SimGlobalReset. Recall that what SimGlobalReset does is to simulate a global reset on the PLD. It is always a good idea to use this initially just to ensure that you have a totally reset simulation before you start to drive signals.
Double click on all of the signals (there will be a red checkmark to indicate selection). Then click on CLOSE at the bottom of the screen.

Step 2:
Now click on Signals -> Add Stimulators in the menu bar at the top of the simulator screen. A box that looks like a keyboard will open. Click on the signal "CLR" in the upper-left portion of the screen and then on the "C" on the keyboard (on the screen). Next click on CLK in the signal list and then on the oval under the red zero on the Bc: line in the stimulator box. Then click on "SimGlobalReset" and then on the keyboard click on "R". We can now drive the inputs and the global reset. Pressing the "R" key will toggle the reset and pressing the "C" key will toggle the "CLR" input to the counter.

Step 3:
Toggle the "R" and the clear signals and then click on the "footsteps" in the menu bar at the top of the screen. You should be able to see the counter counting up and then down.
Hint: Move the signals Y0, Y1, Y2, etc. to be under each other to be able to see the "ripple" effect of the counter. You can easily do this by holding the left mouse button down over the signal to be moved, and releasing it when you have it where you want it in the list.

Step 4:
Now you can physically verify this design by implementing it as in the "Quick Start OR-Gate lab."

Downloading and Testing Your Design

Step 5:
The next step is to download the design to the board as in the "Quick Start OR-Gate lab."

Step 6:
To test the Back-and-Forth Flasher design, use the switches on the board to drive "CLR" low and observe the LEDs and the 7-segment LED. Since there are only eight LEDs, we have also used the 7-segment LEDs for the other eight signals. Refer to your lab book to verify which pins are connected to which LED segments.

Step 7:
Explain in your own words what happens when the "CLR" signal is high.

_____

_____

_____

_____

_____

Step 8:
Give a brief explanation of how the circuit works explaining why the circuit reacts the way it does.

_____

_____

_____

_____

_____

Experiment 11
Seven-Segment Display Lab

Introduction

The purpose of this lab is to build, simulate and download a 7-segment display circuit using the Xilinx Foundation tools and Digilab SpartanXL board.

Objectives

After completing this lab, students will be able to:
- Demonstrate the operation of the circuit described.
- Perform a simple functional and timing simulation using the integrated simulation tool

Preliminary Procedure

Follow the same steps as in the "Quick Start OR-Gate lab" to set up the lab board.

Procedure

Create a new design with the Xilinx Foundation Series Schematic and name the design SevenSeg. Consult the pin table for the specific board you are using to determine where to lock the input and output pins.
You want to create a design that looks like Figure 1:

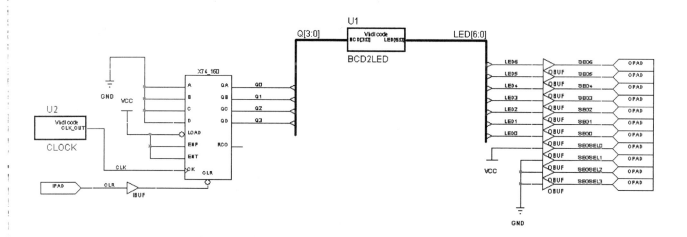

Seven-segment LED display/driver

Figure 1

1) The "BCD2LED" symbol and "CLK_OUT" symbol are custom symbols created with the HDL wizard and are written in VHDL code. If you are learning VHDL, your professor will

have already assigned the "Using Hardware Design Languages with Xilinx tools lab." If you are not learning VHDL at this time, then you will be provided with these symbols a "black boxes" in the custom library. For convenience, the code for these symbols (as well as the entire design is given in both VHDL and Verilog HDLs at the end of this lab. Unless you are studying HDLs you don't need to know much more about this symbol, but if you want to see the design code, first click in the "H" icon and then click on the symbol. To get back up to the top-level schematic, right-click on the mouse and then select "Hierarchy Pop".

2) To connect the symbol to the wires, this schematic uses "busses". These are simply a way of drawing several wires as one and saves a lot of time if you need more than 4 wires into a symbol that are all related such as address or data lines. To draw a bus connection, use the bus icon.

3) Then you have to name the busses such that they have enough names (such as D0, D1, D2 etc.) to satisfy the number of wires that are being represented. You can do this by double-clicking on the bus itself and a window will open that already has the bus range (number of wires) on it and you will have to name it. In this case the bus was named "LED[6:0]".

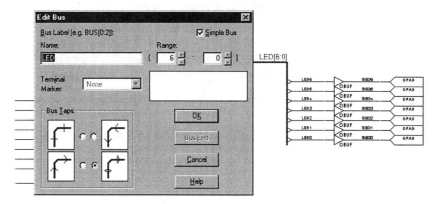

Seven-segment LED display/driver

4) Once you finish creating the desired schematic, make sure to save it. Click **File → Save**. Then return to the Foundation Project Manager (press **<Alt>** + **<Tab>** to task switch).

5) The design entry is finished.

6) Next you need to implement the design the same way as in the "Quick Start OR-Gate lab."

7) Click on the Implementation icon in the Project Manager window and follow the same procedure as in previous labs.

HDL Alternative

Here is the code for the lab in VDHL. Follow the design flow in the "Using Hardware Design Languages (HDLs) with Xilinx tools" tutorial. Don't forget to lock the pins in the ".ucf" file.

This file is the VHDL code for the "OSC4" component in the Xilinx library. This code can be reused in any design. The name of the file is "CLOCK".

```
library IEEE;
use IEEE.std_logic_1164.all;
use IEEE.std_logic_unsigned.all;

entity clock is
    port (
        clk_out: inout STD_LOGIC
    );
end clock;

architecture rtl of clock is
    component OSC4 is
        port (
            F8M: out STD_LOGIC;
            F500K: out STD_LOGIC;
            F16K: out STD_LOGIC;
            F490: out STD_LOGIC;
            F15: out STD_LOGIC
        );
    end component;

    constant tune: STD_LOGIC_VECTOR(3 downto 0) := "0110";
    signal clk: STD_LOGIC;
begin
    spartan_osc4: OSC4
        port map (F15 => clk);

    clock_divide: process(clk)
        variable count: STD_LOGIC_VECTOR(3 downto 0);
    begin
        if rising_edge(clk) then
            if (count = tune) then
                count := "0000";
                clk_out <= not clk_out;
            else
                count := count + 1;
```

```
            end if;
          end if;

      end process clock_divide;
end rtl;
```

This next file is the VHDL code for the BCD-to-Seven-Segment Decoder and is called "BCD2LED". This file can also be reused in other designs.

```vhdl
library IEEE;
use IEEE.std_logic_1164.all;

entity bcd2led is
   port (
      bcd: in STD_LOGIC_VECTOR (3 downto 0);
      led: out STD_LOGIC_VECTOR (6 downto 0)
      );
end bcd2led;

architecture bcd2led_arch of bcd2led is
begin
  with bcd select
       led <= "1111001" when "0001",
              "0100100" when "0010",
              "0110000" when "0011",
              "0011001" when "0100",
              "0010010" when "0101",
              "0000010" when "0110",
              "1111000" when "0111",
              "0000000" when "1000",
              "0010000" when "1001",
              "0001000" when "1010",
              "1000000" when others;
end bcd2led_arch;
```

Here is the code for the exact same design using the Verilog language. First the "CLOCK" file.

```verilog
module clock (CLK_OUT) ;  // Module declaration
   output CLK_OUT;         // Inout declarations

   reg CLK_OUT;            // CLK_OUT declared as reg
   reg osc4_clk;           // Other internal regs
   reg int_clk;
```

```verilog
reg int_clk_out;
reg [3:0] count;
parameter tune = 4'd 6;        // Parameter (constant)

OSC4 spartan_osc4(.F15(osc4_clk));  // Module OSC4 defined within the
                                    // Spartan chip
BUFG bufg_1(.I(osc4_clk), .O(int_clk));  // Internal Clock Buffer

always @(posedge int_clk)// Always run on pos edge of clock
   begin: clock_divide
      if (count == tune)      // Flip the inout clk if the count
         begin           // equal tune and reset the count
            count = 0;
            int_clk_out = ~int_clk_out;
         end
      else
         count = count + 1;  // Otherwise increment the count
   end

BUFG bufg_2(.I(int_clk_out), .O(CLK_OUT));  // Output Clock Buffer
Endmodule
```

Here is the "SEVENSEG" file in Verilog code.

```verilog
module SevenSeg (CLR, SEG, SEGSEL) ;   // Module declaration (with inputs/outputs)
   input CLR;                 // Input declaration
   output [6:0] SEG;          // Output declaration
   output [3:0] SEGSEL;

   reg [6:0] SEG;             // SEG declared as a reg
   reg clk;                   // Internal clock

   parameter LED_zero=7'b 1000000,
        LED_one=7'b 1111001,
        LED_two=7'b 0100100,
        LED_three=7'b 0110000,
        LED_four=7'b 0011001,
        LED_five=7'b 0010010,
        LED_six=7'b 0000010,
        LED_seven=7'b 1111000,
        LED_eight=7'b 0000000,
        LED_nine=7'b 0010000;

   parameter S0=4'd 0, S1=4'd 1, S2=4'd 2, S3=4'd 3,  // States defs
        S4=4'd 4, S5=4'd 5, S6=4'd 6, S7=4'd 7,  // for FSM
        S8=4'd 8, S9=4'd 9;
```

60

```verilog
reg [3:0] cs_BCD, ns_BCD;          // Current state, next state

assign SEGSEL = 4'b 0001;

clock generate_clock(clk);  // Internal clock generator module

always @(posedge clk or negedge CLR)   // Always runs on rising edge
  begin: change_cs                      // of clock or reset
    if (!CLR)                           // reset if true (1)
      cs_BCD = S0;
    else
      cs_BCD = ns_BCD;                  // current to the next state
  end

always @(cs_BCD)                                // Always run on change in current
  begin: change_out_ns
    case (cs_BCD)                               // FSM case selection based on
      S0: begin                         // the defined parameters
          ns_BCD = S1;                  // Includes the output assignment
          SEG = LED_zero;
        end
      S1: begin
          ns_BCD = S2;
          SEG = LED_one;
        end
      S2: begin
          ns_BCD = S3;
          SEG = LED_two;
        end
      S3: begin
          ns_BCD = S4;
          SEG = LED_three;
        end
      S4: begin
          ns_BCD = S5;
          SEG = LED_four;
        end
      S5: begin
          ns_BCD = S6;
          SEG = LED_five;
        end
      S6: begin
          ns_BCD = S7;
          SEG = LED_six;
        end
      S7: begin
```

```
            ns_BCD = S8;
            SEG = LED_seven;
         end
      S8: begin
            ns_BCD = S9;
            SEG = LED_eight;
         end
      S9: begin
            ns_BCD = S0;
            SEG = LED_nine;
         end
      default:
         begin
            ns_BCD = 4'b xxxx;
            SEG = 7'b xxxxxxx;
         end
      endcase
   end
endmodule
```

Briefly describe the similarities and differences between the VHDL and Verilog versions of
the design:

_____

_____

_____

_____

_____

Activity Sheet Experiment 11
Seven-Segment Display Lab

Name: _____

Date: _____

Using the Simulator

Step 1:
To simulate the operation of the 7-segment display, first click on the SIM icon in the menu bar at the top of the schematic screen. The Logic Simulator will open.

Click on Signal -> Add Signals in the menu bar at the top of the simulator screen. Here you can decide which signals to drive and observe during the simulation. Note that the signals available are CLK and CLR, as well as the outputs: SEG6-SEG0 (from the schematic) and something called SimGlobalReset. Recall that what SimGlobalReset does is to simulate a global reset on the PLD. It is always a good idea to use this initially just to ensure that you have a totally reset simulation before you start to drive signals.
Double-click on all of the signals (there will be a red checkmark to indicate selection). Then click on CLOSE at the bottom of the screen.

Step 2:
Now click on Signals -> Add Stimulators in the menu bar at the top of the simulator screen. A box that looks like a keyboard will open. Click on the signal "CLK" in the upper-left portion of the screen and then on the Bc: 1 yellow ball on the keyboard (on the screen). For CLR, using the letter "C". Then click on "SimGlobalReset" and then on the keyboard click on "R". We can now drive the inputs and the global reset. Pressing the "R" key will toggle the reset and pressing the "C" key will toggle the "CLR" input to the circuit.

Step 3:
Toggle the "R" and the input signals and then click on the "footsteps" in the menu bar at the top of the screen. Verify that the outputs follow the truth table in the text.

Step 4:
You can perform a timing simulation of this same design by simply changing the pull-down menu in the menu bar from "Functional" to "Timing".

Now you can physically verify this design by downloading and testing it as in the "Quick Start OR-Gate lab."

Downloading and Testing Your Design

Step 5: Download the design to the board as in the "Quick Start OR-Gate lab."

Step 6:
To test the 7-segment design, use the switch on the board to toggle the "CLR" signal and observe the 7-segment display. The display should count from 0-9. If it looks like it is just being lit up dimly, then it is counting but very fast. You can either input a slower clock or use an oscilloscope to verify the output. Refer to your lab book to verify which pins are connected to the switches and 7-segment display.

Step 7:
Explain in your own words what a wire "bus" is.

_____

_____

_____

_____

Step 8:
Give a brief explanation of how the circuit works, explaining why the circuit reacts the way it does.

_____

_____

_____

_____

Experiment 12 Basic Encoders Lab

Introduction

The purpose of this lab is to build, simulate, and download two basic encoders using the Xilinx Foundation tools and Digilab SpartanXL board.

Objectives

After completing this lab, students will be able to:
- Demonstrate the truth-table operation of the two basic encoders described.
- Perform a simple functional simulation using the integrated simulation tool.

Preliminary Procedure

Follow the same steps as in the "Quick Start OR-Gate lab" to set up the lab board.

Procedure

Create a new design with the Xilinx Foundation Series Schematic and name the design Encoders. Consult the pin table for the specific board you are using to determine where to lock the input and output pins.
You want to create a design in two sheets that looks like Figures 1&2:

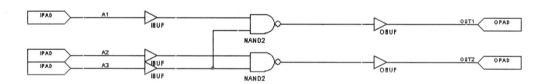

Basic Encoder Circuit (a)

Figure 1

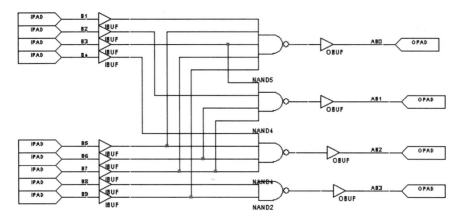

Basic Encoder Circuit (b)

Figure 2

1) Once you finish creating the desired schematic, make sure to save it. <u>Click</u> **File → Save**. Then return to the Foundation Project Manager (press **<Alt>** + **<Tab>** to task switch).

2) The design entry is finished.

Activity Sheet Experiment 12
Basic Encoder Lab

Name: _____

Date: _____

Using the Simulator

Step 1:

This is another chance to practice with the Aldec™ logic simulation tool integrated with the Xilinx software. To simulate the operation of the encoders, first click on the SIM icon in the menu bar at the top of the schematic screen. The Logic Simulator will open.

Click on Signal -> Add Signals in the menu bar at the top of the simulator screen. Here you can decide which signals to drive and observe during the simulation. Note that the signals available are 1A, 2A,…B1, B2 etc. as well as the five outputs: Y and Output1 through 4, (from the schematic) and something called SimGlobalReset. Recall that what SimGlobalReset does is to simulate a global reset on the PLD. It is always a good idea to use this initially just to ensure that you have a totally reset simulation before you start to drive signals.

Double-click on all of the signals (there will be a red checkmark to indicate selection). Then click on CLOSE at the bottom of the screen.

Step 2:

Now click on Signals -> Add Stimulators in the menu bar at the top of the simulator screen. A box that looks like a keyboard will open. Click on the signal "A" in the upper-left portion of the screen and then on the "A" on the keyboard (on the screen). Do the same for B, C, AA, and BB, using letters from the keyboard of your choice. Then click on "SimGlobalReset" and then on the keyboard click on "R". We can now drive the inputs and the global reset.

Pressing the "R" key will toggle the reset and pressing the "A" key will toggle the "A" input to the AND gate in the first encoder.

Step 3:

Toggle the "R" and the input signals and then click on the "footsteps" in the menu bar at the top of the screen. Verify that the truth tables are valid.

Now you can physically verify this design by implementing it as in the "Quick Start OR-Gate lab."

Downloading and Testing Your Design

Step 4: The next step is to download the design to the board as in the "Quick Start OR-Gate lab."

Step 5: To test the encoders design, use the switches on the board and observe the LEDs. Refer to your lab book to verify which pins are connected to the switches and LEDs.

Step 6: Explain in your own words what encoders are used for.

_____

_____

_____

_____

_____

Step 7: Give a brief explanation of how the circuit works, explaining why the circuit reacts the way it does.

_____

_____

_____

_____

_____

Experiment 13
Keypad Encoders Lab

Introduction

The purpose of this lab is to build, simulate and download a basic keypad encoder using the Xilinx Foundation tools and Digilab SpartanXL board.

Objectives

After completing this lab, students will be able to:
- Demonstrate the truth-table operation of the two basic encoders described.
- Perform a simple functional simulation using the integrated simulation tool.

Preliminary Procedure

Follow the same steps as in the "Quick Start OR-Gate lab" to set up the lab board.

Procedure

Create a new design with the Xilinx Foundation Series Schematic and name the design Keypad. Consult the pin table for the specific board you are using to determine where to lock the input and output pins.
You want to create a design in two sheets that looks like Figure 1:

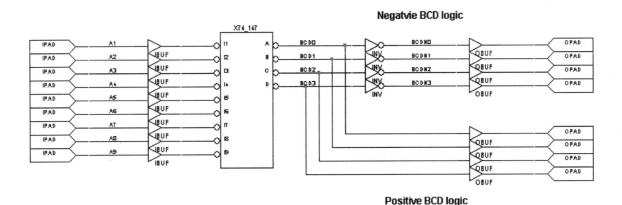

Keypad Encoder Circuit

Figure 1

1) Once you finish creating the desired schematic, make sure to save it. <u>Click</u> **File → Save**. Then return to the Foundation Project Manager (press **\<Alt\>** + **\<Tab\>** to task switch).

2) The design entry is finished.

Note: Depending upon which lab board you are using, you may or may not be able to lock all of the input pins to switches or buttons. If this is the case, I recommend that you use the software to tie the unused pins to either VCC or ground and analyze your results accordingly.

Activity Sheet Experiment 13
Keypad Encoders Lab

Name: _____

Date: _____

Using the Simulator

Step 1: This is another chance to practice with the Aldec™ logic simulation tool integrated with the Xilinx software. To simulate the operation of the encoders, first click on the SIM icon in the menu bar at the top of the schematic screen. The Logic Simulator will open.

Click on Signal -> Add Signals in the menu bar at the top of the simulator screen. Here you can decide which signals to drive and observe during the simulation. Note that the signals available are I1 to I9, as well as the eight outputs: Neg 0 through Neg3 and POS0 through POS3 (from the schematic), and something called SimGlobalReset. Recall that what SimGlobalReset does is to simulate a global reset on the PLD. It is always a good idea to use this initially just to ensure that you have a totally reset simulation before you start to drive signals.
Double click on all of the signals (there will be a red checkmark to indicate selection). Then click on CLOSE at the bottom of the screen.

Step 2: Now click on Signals -> Add Stimulators in the menu bar at the top of the simulator screen. A box that looks like a keyboard will open. Click on the signal "A" in the upper left portion of the screen and then on the "I1" on the keyboard (on the screen). Do the same for I2, I3, and so on, using letters from the (screen) keyboard of your choice. Then click on "SimGlobalReset" and then on the keyboard click on "R". We can now drive the inputs and the global reset. Pressing the "R" key will toggle the reset and pressing the "A" key will toggle the "I1" input circuit.

Step 3: Toggle the "R" and the input signals and then click on the "footsteps" in the menu bar at the top of the screen. Verify that the truth tables from the text are valid.

Step 4: Now you can physically verify this design by implementing it as in the "Quick Start OR-Gate lab."

Downloading and Testing Your Design

Step 5: Download the design to the board as in the "Quick Start OR-Gate lab."

Step 6: To test the keypad encoders design, use the switches on the board and observe the LEDs. Refer to your lab book to verify which pins are connected to the switches and LEDs.

Step 7: Give a brief explanation of how the circuit works explaining why the circuit reacts the way it does.

_____

_____

_____

_____

_____

Experiment 14 Troubleshooting Encoder/Decoders

Introduction

The purpose of this lab is to build and troubleshoot an encoder/decoder using the Xilinx Foundation tools and Digilab SpartanXL board.

Objectives

After completing this lab, students will be able to:
- Demonstrate the truth-table operation of the two basic encoders described.
- Perform a simple functional simulation using the integrated simulation tool.

Preliminary Procedure

Follow the same steps as in the "Quick Start OR-Gate lab" to set up the lab board.

Procedure

Create a new design with the Xilinx Foundation Series Schematic and name the design Troubleshoot . Consult the pin table for the specific board you are using to determine where to lock the input and output pins.
You want to create a design that looks like Figure 1:
(Note: For information on the "VHDL code" module, see the 7-segment LED driver lab.)

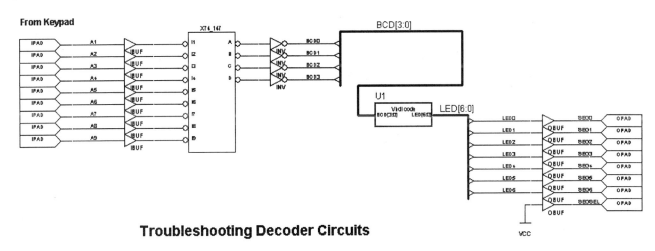

Troubleshooting Decoder Circuits

Figure 1

1) Once you finish creating the desired schematic, make sure to save it. <u>Click</u> **File → Save**. Then return to the Foundation Project Manager (press **<Alt>** + **<Tab>** to task switch).

2) The design entry is finished.

You will note that the design once again uses the "BCD2LED" VHDL file. It is reproduced here for your convenience:

library IEEE;
use IEEE.std_logic_1164.all;

entity bcd2led is
  port (
    bcd: in STD_LOGIC_VECTOR (3 downto 0);
    led: out STD_LOGIC_VECTOR (6 downto 0)
    );
end bcd2led;

architecture bcd2led_arch of bcd2led is
begin
  with bcd select
      led <= "1111001" when "0001",
          "0100100" when "0010",
          "0110000" when "0011",
          "0011001" when "0100",
          "0010010" when "0101",
          "0000010" when "0110",
          "1111000" when "0111",
          "0000000" when "1000",
          "0010000" when "1001",
          "0001000" when "1010",
          "1000000" when others;
end bcd2led_arch;

Activity Sheet Experiment 14
Troubleshooting Encoder/Decoders

Name: _____

Date: _____

Using the Simulator

Step 1:
This is another chance to practice with the Aldec™ logic simulation tool integrated with the Xilinx software. To simulate the operation of the keypad encoder, first click on the SIM icon in the menu bar at the top of the schematic screen. The Logic Simulator will open.

Click on Signal -> Add Signals in the menu bar at the top of the simulator screen. Here you can decide which signals to drive and observe during the simulation. Note that the signals available are A1-A9 as well as the eight outputs: SEG0 through SEG6 (from the schematic), and something called SimGlobalReset. Recall that what SimGlobalReset does is to simulate a global reset on the PLD. It is always a good idea to use this initially just to ensure that you have a totally reset simulation before you start to drive signals.
Double click on all of the signals (there will be a red checkmark to indicate selection). Then click on CLOSE at the bottom of the screen.

Step 2:
Now click on Signals -> Add Stimulators in the menu bar at the top of the simulator screen. A box that looks like a keyboard will open. Click on the signal "A1" in the upper-left portion of the screen and then on the "A" on the keyboard (on the screen). Do the same for A2-A9, using letters from the keyboard of your choice. Then click on "SimGlobalReset" and then on the keyboard click on "R". We can now drive the inputs and the global reset. Pressing the "R" key will toggle the reset and pressing the "A" key will toggle the "A" input to the encoder.

Step 3:
Toggle the "R" and the input signals and then click on the "footsteps" in the menu bar at the top of the screen.

Now you can physically verify this design by implementing it as in the "Quick Start OR-Gate lab."

Downloading and Testing Your Design

Step 4: Download the design to the board as in the "Quick Start OR-Gate lab."

Step 5: To test the encoder/decoder use the switches on the board and observe the 7-segment display. Refer to your lab book to verify which pins are connected to the switches and LEDs.

Step 6: If the encoder did not work at first, explain in your own words what you did to determine that it does not work, and how you fixed it.

_____

_____

_____

_____

_____

Step 7: Give a brief explanation of how you fixed the circuit so it worked properly.

_____

_____

_____

_____

_____

Experiment 15 Basic Multiplexer Lab

Introduction

The purpose of this lab is to build, simulate, and download a basic multiplexer circuit using the Xilinx Foundation tools and Digilab SpartanXL board.

Objectives

After completing this lab, students will be able to:
- Demonstrate the operation of the basic multiplexer described.
- Perform a simple functional and timing simulation using the integrated simulation tool.

Preliminary Procedure

Follow the same steps as in the "Quick Start OR-Gate lab" to set up the lab board.

Procedure

Create a new design with the Xilinx Foundation Series Schematic and name the design Mux. Consult the pin table for the specific board you are using to determine where to lock the input and output pins.
You want to create a design that looks like Figure 1:

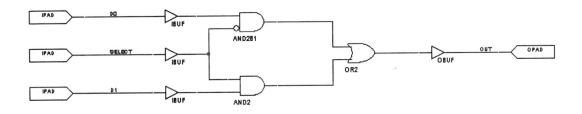

Basic Multiplexer
Figure 1

1) Once you finish creating the desired schematic, make sure to save it. <u>Click</u> **File → Save**. Then return to the Foundation Project Manager (press **<Alt>** + **<Tab>** to task switch).

2) The design entry is finished.

3) Next you need to implement the design the same way as in the Quick Start OR-Gate lab.

4) Click on the Implementation icon in the Project Manager window and follow the same procedure as in previous labs.

Activity Sheet Experiment 15
Basic Multiplexer Lab

Name: _____

Date: _____

Using the Simulator

Step 1:
To simulate the operation of the multiplexer, first click on the SIM icon in the menu bar at the top of the schematic screen. The Logic Simulator will open.

Step 2:
Click on Signal -> Add Signals in the menu bar at the top of the simulator screen. Here you can decide which signals to drive and observe during the simulation. Note that the signals available are D0, D1, and S, as well as the output: Y (from the schematic) and something called SimGlobalReset. Recall that what SimGlobalReset does is to simulate a global reset on the PLD. It is always a good idea to use this initially just to ensure that you have a totally reset simulation before you start to drive signals.
Double-click on all of the signals (there will be a red checkmark to indicate selection). Then click on CLOSE at the bottom of the screen.

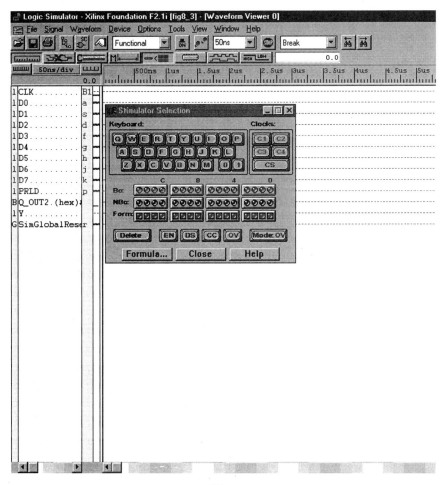

Step 3:
Now click on Signals -> Add Stimulators in the menu bar at the top of the simulator screen. A box that looks like a keyboard will open. Click on the signal "D0" in the upper-left portion of the screen and then on the "D" on the keyboard (on the screen). Do the same for D1 using the letter "F" and also for signal S, using the letter "S". Then click on "SimGlobalReset" and then on the keyboard click on "R". We can now drive the inputs and the global reset. Pressing the "R" key will toggle the reset and pressing the "D" key will toggle the "D0" input to the multiplexer and so on.

Step 4:
Toggle the "R" and the input signals and then click on the "footsteps" in the menu bar at the top of the screen. Complete the following truth table:

S	Output
0	Y=
1	Y=

Step 5:
You can perform a timing simulation of this same design by simply changing the pull-down menu in the menu bar from "Functional" to "Timing".

Step 6:
Now you can physically verify this design by downloading and testing it as in the "Quick Start OR-Gate lab."

Downloading and Testing Your Design

Step 7: Download the design to the board as in the "Quick Start OR-Gate lab."

Step 8: To test the multiplexer design, use the switches on the board and observe the LEDs. Refer to your lab book to verify which pins are connected to the switches and LEDs.

Step 9: Explain in your own words the purpose of the Select line.

_____

_____

_____

_____

_____

Step 10: Give a brief explanation of how the circuit works, explaining why the circuit reacts the way it does.

_____

_____

_____

_____

_____

Experiment 16
Parallel-to-Serial Data Conversion Lab

Introduction

The purpose of this lab is to build, simulate, and download a parallel-to-serial data conversion circuit using the Xilinx Foundation tools and Digilab SpartanXL board.

Objectives

After completing this lab, students will be able to:

- Demonstrate the operation of a parallel-to-serial data converter
- Generate a custom counter using LogiBLOX™.
- Perform functional and timing simulations of the parallel-to-serial conversion circuit using the integrated simulation tool.

Preliminary Procedure

Follow the same steps as in the "Quick Start OR-Gate lab" to set up the lab board.

Procedure

Create a new design with the Xilinx Foundation Series Schematic and name the design Flasher. Consult the pin table for the specific board you are using to determine where to lock the input and output pins.
You want to create a design that looks like this:

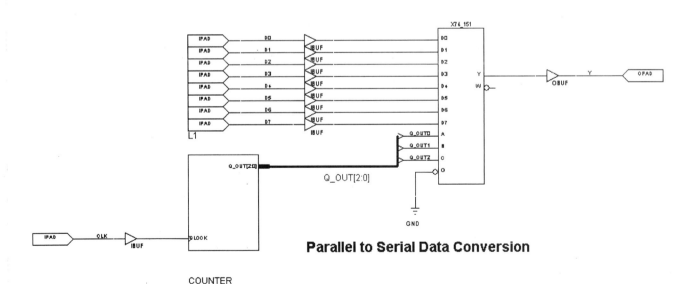

Parallel to Serial Data Conversion

COUNTER

3 Bit Counter generated using LogicBlox

5) The X74_151 component is straightforward as in previous labs. The counter, however, is a custom designed 3-bit counter using an integrated tool called LogiBLOX. To start the LogiBLOX tool and generate the counter, first select Tools→LogiBLOX Module Generator from the pull down menus at the top of the Project Manager page.

6) Next select "Counters" from the Module Type box and type "3-bit" in the Module Name box. Type "3" in the Bus Width box. Set up the rest of the parameters as shown in Figure 2.

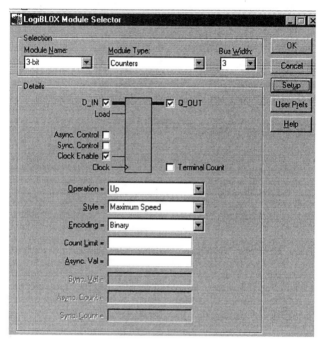

Figure 2

7) When the parameters are set as shown, click on OK and the counter will automatically be created for you. Then simply pick the 3-bit module out of the library the same way you selected the X74_151.

8) Once you finish creating the desired schematic, make sure to save it. Click **File → Save**. Then return to the Foundation Project Manager (press **<Alt> + <Tab>** to task switch).

9) The design entry is finished. Click on the Implementation icon in the Project Manager to place and route the design.

HDL Alternative

Here is the code for the lab in VDHL. Follow the design flow in the "Using Hardware Design Languages (HDLs) with Xilinx tools" tutorial. Don't forget to lock the pins in the ".ucf" file.

Here is the VHDL code for the 3-bit counter in this design:

```
--------------------------------------------------------
-- LogiBLOX COUNTER Module "counter_3bit"
-- Created by LogiBLOX version C.22
--    on Thu Aug 17 16:24:08 2000
-- Attributes
--    MODTYPE = COUNTER
--    BUS_WIDTH = 3
--    STYLE = MAX_SPEED
--    OPTYPE = UP
--    ENCODING = BINARY
--------------------------------------------------------
-- This is a behavioral model only and cannot be synthesized.
--------------------------------------------------------
LIBRARY IEEE;
USE IEEE.std_logic_1164.ALL;
LIBRARY logiblox;
USE logiblox.mvlutil.ALL;
USE logiblox.mvlarith.ALL;
USE logiblox.logiblox.ALL;

ENTITY counter_3bit IS
  PORT(
    CLOCK: IN std_logic;
    Q_OUT: OUT std_logic_vector(2 DOWNTO 0));
END counter_3bit;

ARCHITECTURE sim OF counter_3bit IS
  SIGNAL START_PULSE: std_logic := '1';
BEGIN
  PROCESS
    VARIABLE VD_IN: std_logic_vector(2 DOWNTO 0);
    VARIABLE VLOAD: std_logic;
    VARIABLE VUP_DN: std_logic;
    VARIABLE VCLK_EN: std_logic;
    VARIABLE VCLOCK: std_logic;
    VARIABLE VASYNC_CTRL: std_logic;
    VARIABLE VSYNC_CTRL: std_logic;
```

```vhdl
      VARIABLE VQ_OUT: std_logic_vector(2 DOWNTO 0);
      VARIABLE VTERM_CNT: std_logic;
      VARIABLE lowest_count: std_logic_vector(2 DOWNTO 0) := ('0','0','0');
      BEGIN
       VLOAD := '0';
       VUP_DN := '1';
       VASYNC_CTRL := '0';
       VSYNC_CTRL := '0';
       VUP_DN := '1';
       IF(
       (CLOCK'EVENT AND stdbit2mvl(CLOCK)='1' AND
stdbit2mvl(CLOCK'LAST_VALUE)='0')
        OR ( stdbit2mvl(START_PULSE)='1')
       ) THEN
       xb_counter(
            START_PULSE,
            VUP_DN,
            VASYNC_CTRL,
            ('0','0','0'),
            VSYNC_CTRL,
            ('0','0','0'),
            VLOAD,
            VD_IN,
            ('1','1','1'),
            VQ_OUT);
       Q_OUT <= VQ_OUT;
       ELSIF(
        (stdbit2mvl(CLOCK) = 'X')
       ) THEN
         VQ_OUT := ('X','X','X');
         Q_OUT <= VQ_OUT;
       END IF;
       IF (START_PULSE='1') THEN
         START_PULSE <= '0' AFTER 1 ns;
       END IF;
       WAIT ON CLOCK, START_PULSE;
     END PROCESS;
END sim;
```

Here is the VHDL code for the storage element:

```vhdl
library IEEE;
use IEEE.std_logic_1164.all;
use IEEE.std_logic_unsigned.all;  -- Added this IEEE unsigned library
                   -- to use CONV_INTEGER function
entity p2s is                -- which converts std_logic_vectors
```

```
port (                    -- to integers
   CLK: IN STD_LOGIC;
   D: in STD_LOGIC_VECTOR (7 downto 0);
   Y: out STD_LOGIC
);
end p2s;

architecture rtl of p2s is
   component counter_3bit        -- Component declaration from
      PORT(                 -- LogicBLOX counter component
         CLOCK: IN std_logic;
         Q_OUT: OUT std_logic_vector(2 DOWNTO 0)
      );
   end component;

   signal count: STD_LOGIC_VECTOR(2 downto 0);  -- The count signal
begin
   generate_count: counter_3bit  -- The counter with the internal clk
      port map (CLK, count);    -- signal and output count value

   Y <= D(CONV_INTEGER(count));  -- Converts count to integer and
end rtl;                   -- assigns the bit slice to Y
```

Now the same design is presented in the Verilog HDL:

```
module p2s (CLK, D, Y);
   input CLK;
   input [7:0] D;
   output Y;

   reg Y;
   reg [2:0] count;

   counter_3bit generate_count(.CLOCK(CLK), .Q_OUT(count));  // 3-bit binary
                                 // LogiBLOX counter
   always @(count or D)  // activate process on changing of count or D
      begin: assign_serial_bit
         Y = D[count];    // Assign the correct bit slice determined by
      end            // count
endmodule
```

Which HDL language is more efficient for this design? Why?

_____

_____

Activity Sheet Experiment 16
Parallel-to-Serial Data Conversion Lab

Name: _____

Date: _____

Using the Simulator

Step 1: This is another chance to practice with the Aldec™ logic simulation tool integrated with the Xilinx software. To simulate the operation of the conversion circuit, first click on the SIM icon in the menu bar at the top of the schematic screen. The Logic Simulator will open.

Step 2: Next, click on Signal -> Add Signals in the menu bar at the top of the simulator screen. Here you can decide which signals to drive and observe during the simulation. Note that the signals available are only CLK and PRLD as well as the eight inputs: D0-D7 and the single output: Y (from the schematic), and something called SimGlobalReset. Recall that what SimGlobalReset does is to simulate a global reset on the PLD. It is always a good idea to use this initially just to ensure that you have a totally reset simulation before you start to drive signals. Double click on all of the signals (there will be a red checkmark to indicate selection). Then click on CLOSE at the bottom of the screen.

Step 3: Now click on Signals -> Add Stimulators in the menu bar at the top of the simulator screen. A box that looks like a keyboard will open. Click on the signals and add the stimulus as shown in Figure 3. Remember that Y and the Q_out bus are outputs and therefore are not driven. Next click on CLK in the signal list and then on the oval under the red zero on the Bc: line in the stimulator box. Then click on "SimGlobalReset" and then on the keyboard click on "R". We can now drive the inputs and the global reset. Pressing the "R" key will toggle the reset and pressing the "P" key will toggle the "PRLD" input to the counter.

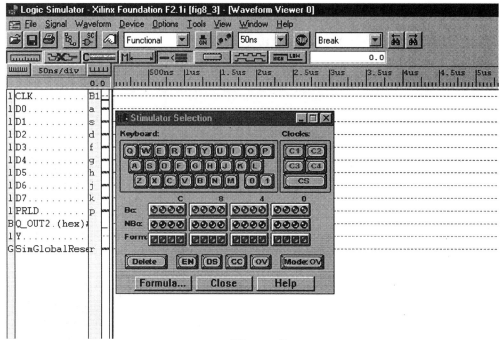

Figure 3

Step 4: Toggle the "R" and the input signals and then click on the "footsteps" in the menu bar at the top of the screen. Based on your D inputs you should be able to duplicate the Y output as shown in the text.

Step 5: If you would like to perform a timing simulation of this design, simply change the pull-down dialog box at the top of the screen from Functional to Timing. You will then be able to see some glitching as you speed up the clock and it takes time for the signals to settle down.

Step 6: Now you can physically verify this design by implementing it as in the "Quick Start OR-Gate lab."

Downloading and Testing Your Design

Step 7: Download the design to the board as in the "Quick Start OR-Gate lab."

Step 8: To test the parallel-to-serial data circuit, use the switches on the board as the storage registers and observe the LED.

Step 9: Explain in your own words what function the counter provides in the circuit.

_____

_____

_____

_____

_____

Step 10: Give a brief explanation of how the circuit works.

_____

_____

_____

_____

_____

Experiment 17
Logic Function Generator Lab

Introduction

The purpose of this lab is to build, simulate, and download a logic function generator circuit using the Xilinx Foundation tools and Digilab SpartanXL board.

Objectives

After completing this lab, students will be able to:
- Demonstrate the operation of the logic function generator described.
- Perform a simple functional and timing simulation using the integrated simulation tool.

Preliminary Procedure

Follow the same steps as in the "Quick Start OR-Gate lab" to set up the lab board.

Procedure

Create a new design with the Xilinx Foundation Series Schematic and name the design Fcngen. Consult the pin table for the specific board you are using to determine where to lock the input and output pins.
You want to create a design that looks like this:

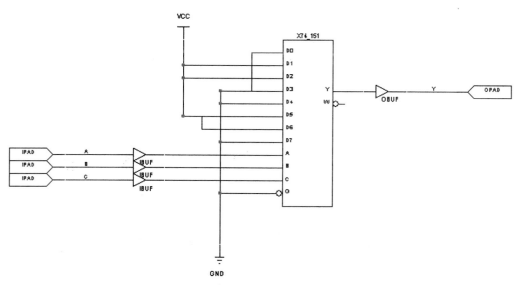

Logic Function Generator

1) Once you finish creating the desired schematic, make sure to save it. <u>Click</u> **File → Save**. Then return to the Foundation Project Manager (press **\<Alt\>** + **\<Tab\>** to task switch).

2) The design entry is finished.

3) Next you need to implement the design the same way as in the Quick Start OR-Gate lab.

4) Click on the Implementation icon in the Project Manager window and follow the same procedure as in previous labs.

Activity Sheet Experiment 17
Logic Function Generator Lab

Name: _____

Date: _____

Using the Simulator

Step 1:
This is another chance to practice with the Aldec™ logic simulation tool integrated with the Xilinx software. To simulate the operation of the conversion circuit, first click on the SIM icon in the menu bar at the top of the schematic screen. The Logic Simulator will open.

Step 2:
Next, click on Signal -> Add Signals in the menu bar at the top of the simulator screen. Here you can decide which signals to drive and observe during the simulation. Note that the signals available are A, B, C, as well as the output Y (from the schematic), and something called SimGlobalReset. Recall that what SimGlobalReset does is to simulate a global reset on the PLD. It is always a good idea to use this initially just to ensure that you have a totally reset simulation before you start to drive signals.
Double-click on all of the signals (there will be a red checkmark to indicate selection). Then click on CLOSE at the bottom of the screen.

Step 3:
Now click on Signals -> Add Stimulators in the menu bar at the top of the simulator screen. A box that looks like a keyboard will open. Click on the signal "A" in the upper-left portion of the screen and then on the "A" on the keyboard (on the screen). Do the same for B and C, using letters from the keyboard of your choice. Then click on "SimGlobalReset" and then on the keyboard click on "R". We can now drive the inputs and the global reset. Pressing the "R" key will toggle the reset and pressing the "A" key will toggle the "A" input logic function generator.

Step 4:
Toggle the "R" and the input signals and then click on the "footsteps" in the menu bar at the top of the screen. Complete the following truth table:

Logic Generator Function Table

Ckt.				Input Selected
C	B	A	Y	
0	0	0		
0	0	1		
0	1	0		
0	1	1		
1	0	0		
1	0	1		
1	1	0		
1	1	1		

Step 5:

You can perform a timing simulation of this same design by simply changing the pull-down menu in the menu bar from "Functional" to "Timing".

Now you can physically verify this design by downloading and testing it as in the "Quick Start OR-Gate lab."

Downloading and Testing Your Design

Step 6:

Download the design to the board as in the "Quick Start OR-Gate lab."

Step 7:

To test the function generator design, use the switches on the board and observe the LEDs. Complete the following truth table and make sure that it is the same as the one you completed in the simulation stage.

Refer to your lab book to verify which pins are connected to the switches and LEDs.

Logic Generator Function Table

Ckt.				Input Selected
C	B	A	Y	
0	0	0		
0	0	1		
0	1	0		
0	1	1		
1	0	0		
1	0	1		
1	1	0		
1	1	1		

Step 8:
In your own words, give a brief explanation of how the circuit works.

_____

_____

_____

_____

_____

Experiment 18 Multiplexed Display Lab

Introduction

The purpose of this lab is to build, simulate, and download a multiplexed display circuit using the Xilinx Foundation tools and Digilab SpartanXL board.

Objectives

After completing this lab, students will be able to:
- Demonstrate the operation of the circuit described.
- Perform a simple functional and timing simulation using the integrated simulation tool.

Preliminary Procedure

Follow the same steps as in the "Quick Start OR-Gate lab" to set up the lab board.

Procedure

Create a new design with the Xilinx Foundation Series Schematic and name the design Display. Consult the pin table for the specific board you are using to determine where to lock the input and output pins.
You want to create a design that looks like this:

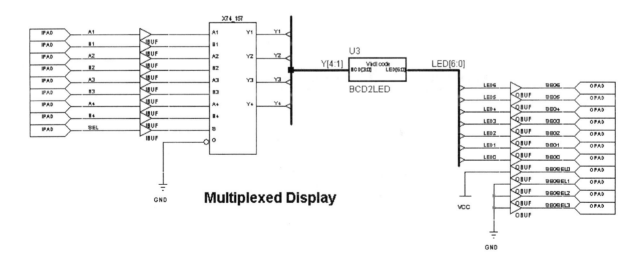

1) The "BCD2LED" symbol is a custom symbol created with the HDL wizard and is written in VHDL code. You don't need to know much more about this symbol, but if you want to see the code, first click in the "H" icon and then click on the symbol. To get back up to the top-level schematic, right-click on the mouse and then on "Hierarchy Pop".

2) To connect the symbol to the wires this schematic uses "busses". These are simply a way of drawing several wires as one and saves a lot of time if you need more than 4 wires into a symbol that are all related such as address or data lines. To draw a bus connection, use the Bus icon.

3) Then you have to name the bus, such that it has enough names (such as D0, D1, D2, etc.) to satisfy the number of wires that are being represented. You can do this by double-clicking on the bus itself and a window will open that already has the bus range (number of wires) on it and you will have to name it. In this case the output bus was named "SEG[6:0].

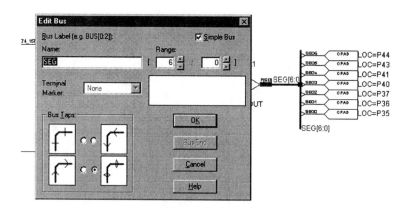

4) Once you finish creating the desired schematic, make sure to save it. Click **File → Save**. Then return to the Foundation Project Manager (press **<Alt>** + **<Tab>** to task switch).

5) The design entry is finished.

6) Next you need to implement the design the same way as in the Quick Start OR-Gate lab.

7) Click on the Implementation icon in the Project Manager window and follow the same procedure as in previous labs.

HDL Alternative

Here is the code for the lab in VDHL. Follow the design flow in the "Using Hardware Design Languages (HDLs) with Xilinx tools" tutorial. Don't forget to lock the pins in the ".ucf" file.

Here is the VHDL code for the design:

```vhdl
library IEEE;
use IEEE.std_logic_1164.all;
use IEEE.std_logic_unsigned.all;

entity display is
    port (
        A: in STD_LOGIC_VECTOR (3 downto 0);
        B: in STD_LOGIC_VECTOR (3 downto 0);
        SEL: in STD_LOGIC;
        SEG: out STD_LOGIC_VECTOR (6 downto 0);
        SEGSEL: out STD_LOGIC_VECTOR(3 downto 0)
    );
end display;

architecture rtl of display is
    constant LED_zero: STD_LOGIC_VECTOR(6 downto 0) := "1000000";
    constant LED_one: STD_LOGIC_VECTOR(6 downto 0) := "1111001";
    constant LED_two: STD_LOGIC_VECTOR(6 downto 0) := "0100100";
    constant LED_three: STD_LOGIC_VECTOR(6 downto 0) := "0110000";
    constant LED_four: STD_LOGIC_VECTOR(6 downto 0) := "0011001";
    constant LED_five: STD_LOGIC_VECTOR(6 downto 0) := "0010010";
    constant LED_six: STD_LOGIC_VECTOR(6 downto 0) := "0000010";
    constant LED_seven: STD_LOGIC_VECTOR(6 downto 0) := "1111000";
    constant LED_eight: STD_LOGIC_VECTOR(6 downto 0) := "0000000";
    constant LED_nine: STD_LOGIC_VECTOR(6 downto 0) := "0010000";

    type LED_type is array (0 to 9) of STD_LOGIC_VECTOR(6 downto 0);
    signal LED: LED_type;
begin
    LED(0) <= LED_zero;   -- Assigned each constant for the LED to
    LED(1) <= LED_one;    -- an array
    LED(2) <= LED_two;
    LED(3) <= LED_three;
    LED(4) <= LED_four;
    LED(5) <= LED_five;
    LED(6) <= LED_six;
    LED(7) <= LED_seven;
```

```
    LED(8) <= LED_eight;
    LED(9) <= LED_nine;

    SEGSEL <= "0001";

    SEG <= LED(CONV_INTEGER(A)) when SEL = '1' -- Converts the std_logic
        else LED(CONV_INTEGER(B));  -- into an index into the LED array
end rtl;                            -- based upon the SEL value
```

Here is the Verilog code for the design:

```
module display (A, B, SEL, SEG, SEGSEL);
    input [3:0] A;
    input [3:0] B;
    input SEL;
    output [6:0] SEG;
    output [3:0] SEGSEL;

    reg [6:0] SEG;
    reg [6:0] LED [0:9];  // Array of LED output constants

    parameter LED_zero=7'b 1000000,
        LED_one=7'b 1111001,
        LED_two=7'b 0100100,
        LED_three=7'b 0110000,
        LED_four=7'b 0011001,
        LED_five=7'b 0010010,
        LED_six=7'b 0000010,
        LED_seven=7'b 1111000,
        LED_eight=7'b 0000000,
        LED_nine=7'b 0010000;

    assign SEGSEL = 4'b 0001;

    always  // An always block which runs constantly (in simulation)
        begin: assign_led_constants  // Assigns constants (ROM) on
            LED[0] = LED_zero;      // power up of chip
            LED[1] = LED_one;
            LED[2] = LED_two;
            LED[3] = LED_three;
            LED[4] = LED_four;
            LED[5] = LED_five;
            LED[6] = LED_six;
            LED[7] = LED_seven;
            LED[8] = LED_eight;
            LED[9] = LED_nine;
```

```verilog
      end

   always @(A or B or SEL)  // Switch the output if A or B or SEL
   begin                    // changes
      if (SEL)
         SEG = LED[A];    // Assign the LED code referenced by A
      else
         SEG = LED[B];    // Assign the LED code referenced by B
   end
endmodule
```

Activity Sheet Experiment 18
Multiplexed Display Lab

Name: _____

Date: _____

Using the Simulator

Step 1:
To simulate the operation of the multiplexed display, first click on the SIM icon in the menu bar at the top of the schematic screen. The Logic Simulator will open.

Step 2:
Next, click on Signal -> Add Signals in the menu bar at the top of the simulator screen. Here you can decide which signals to drive and observe during the simulation. Note that the signals available are A1-A4, B1-B4 and SEL as well as the outputs: SEG[6:0] (from the schematic) and something called SimGlobalReset. Recall that what SimGlobalReset does is to simulate a global reset on the PLD. It is always a good idea to use this initially just to ensure that you have a totally reset simulation before you start to drive signals.
Double-click on all of the signals (there will be a red checkmark to indicate selection). Then click on CLOSE at the bottom of the screen.

Step 3:
Now click on Signals -> Add Stimulators in the menu bar at the top of the simulator screen. A box that looks like a keyboard will open. Click on the signal "A1" in the upper left portion of the screen and then on the "A" on the keyboard (on the screen). Do the same for A2, using the letter "S" and so on for B1-B4 and SEL. Then click on "SimGlobalReset" and then on the keyboard click on "R". We can now drive the inputs and the global reset. Pressing the "R" key will toggle the reset and pressing the "A" key will toggle the "A1" input to the circuit and pressing the "S" key will select the A or B inputs.

Step 4:
Toggle the "R" and the input signals and then click on the "footsteps" in the menu bar at the top of the screen. Verify that the outputs follow the truth tables in the text.

Step 5:
You can perform a timing simulation of this same design by simply changing the pull-down menu in the menu bar from "Functional" to "Timing".

Step 6:
Now you can physically verify this design by downloading and testing it as in the "Quick Start OR-Gate lab."

Downloading and Testing Your Design

Step 7:
Download the design to the board as in the "Quick Start OR-Gate lab."

Step 8:
To test the multiplexed design use the switches on the board and observe the 7-segment display. Refer to your lab book to verify which pins are connected to the switches and display.

Step 9:
Explain in your own words what function the XC74_157 provides in the circuit.

_____

_____

_____

_____

_____

Step 10:
Give a brief explanation of how the circuit works.

_____

_____

_____

_____

_____

Experiment 19 Basic Demultiplexer Lab

Introduction

The purpose of this lab is to build, simulate, and download a basic demultiplexer circuit using the Xilinx Foundation tools and Digilab SpartanXL board.

Objectives

After completing this lab, students will be able to:

- Demonstrate the operation of the demultiplexer described.
- Perform a simple functional and timing simulation using the integrated simulation tool.

Preliminary Procedure

Follow the same steps as in the "Quick Start OR-Gate lab" to set up the lab board.

Procedure

Create a new design with the Xilinx Foundation Series Schematic and name the design Demux. Consult the pin table for the specific board you are using to determine where to lock the input and output pins.
You want to create a design that looks like Figure 1:

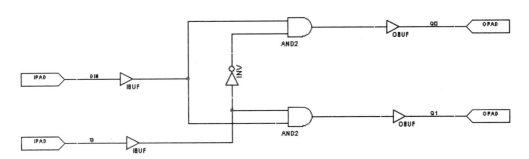

Basic Demultiplexer

Figure 1

1) Once you finish creating the desired schematic, make sure to save it. <u>Click</u> **File → Save**. Then return to the Foundation Project Manager (press **<Alt>** + **<Tab>** to task switch).

2) The design entry is finished.

3) Next you need to implement the design the same way as in the Quick Start OR-Gate lab.

4) Click on the Implementation icon in the Project Manager window and follow the same procedure as in previous labs.

Activity Sheet Experiment 19
Demultiplexer Lab

Name: _____

Date: _____

Using the Simulator

Step 1:
To simulate the operation of the multiplexer, first click on the SIM icon in the menu bar at the top of the schematic screen. The Logic Simulator will open.

Step 2:
Next, click on Signal -> Add Signals in the menu bar at the top of the simulator screen. Here you can decide which signals to drive and observe during the simulation. Note that the signals available are Din and S as well as the outputs: Q0 and Q1 (from the schematic) and something called SimGlobalReset. Recall that what SimGlobalReset does is to simulate a global reset on the PLD. It is always a good idea to use this initially just to ensure that you have a totally reset simulation before you start to drive signals.
Double-click on all of the signals (there will be a red checkmark to indicate selection). Then click on CLOSE at the bottom of the screen.

Step 3:
Now click on Signals -> Add Stimulators in the menu bar at the top of the simulator screen. A box that looks like a keyboard will open. Click on the signal "Din" in the upper-left portion of the screen and then on the "D" on the keyboard (on the screen). Do the same for S, using the letter "S". Then click on "SimGlobalReset" and then on the keyboard click on "R". We can now drive the inputs and the global reset. Pressing the "R" key will toggle the reset and pressing the "D" key will toggle the "Din" input to the demultiplexer and pressing the "S" key will toggle the select line.

Step 4:
Toggle the "R" and the input signals and then click on the "footsteps" in the menu bar at the top of the screen. Complete the following truth table:

S	Output
0	Q0=___
1	Q1=___

You can perform a timing simulation of this same design by simply changing the pull-down menu in the menu bar from "Functional" to "Timing".

Step 5:

Now you can physically verify this design by downloading and testing it as in the "Quick Start OR-Gate lab."

Downloading and Testing Your Design

Step 6:

Download the design to the board as in the "Quick Start OR-Gate lab."

Step 7:

To test the multiplexer design, use the switches on the board and observe the LEDs. Refer to your lab book to verify which pins are connected to the switches and LEDs.

Step 8:

Verify that the truth table you completed in step 4 is valid.

Step 9:

Give a brief explanation of how the circuit works.

_____

_____

_____

_____

_____

Experiment 20 4-to-16 Demultiplexer Lab

Introduction

The purpose of this lab is to build, simulate, and download a 4-to-6 demultiplexer circuit using the Xilinx Foundation tools and Digilab SpartanXL board.

Objectives

After completing this lab, students will be able to:
- Demonstrate the operation of the demultiplexer described.
- Perform a simple functional and timing simulation using the integrated simulation tool.

Preliminary Procedure

Follow the same steps as in the "Quick Start OR-Gate lab" to set up the lab board.

Procedure

Create a new design with the Xilinx Foundation Series Schematic and name the design Demux2. Consult the pin table for the specific board you are using to determine where to lock the input and output pins.
You want to create a design that looks like this:

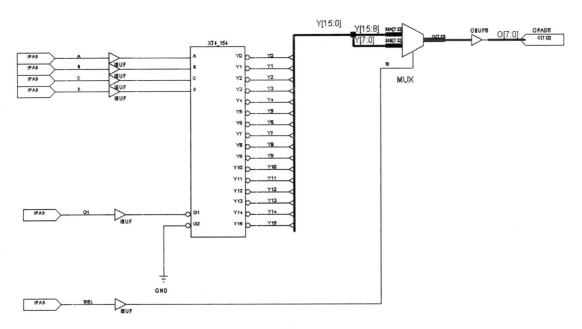

4-to-16 Decoder/Demultiplexer

1) To create the outputs pins using the "OPAD8" symbol, you can "LOC" the pins in the .ucf file. For your convenience we have reproduced the .ucf file below.

```
# Digilab XL Pin Constraints
# August 15, 2000
NET A LOC = P28;
NET B LOC = P27;
NET C LOC = P26;
NET D LOC = P25;
NET G1 LOC = P24;
NET SEL LOC = P23;
NET O<0> LOC = P69;
NET O<1> LOC = P68;
NET O<2> LOC = P67;
NET O<3> LOC = P66;
NET O<4> LOC = P65;
NET O<5> LOC = P62;
NET O<6> LOC = P61;
NET O<7> LOC = P60;
```

2) Once you finish creating the desired schematic, make sure to save it. Click **File → Save**. Then return to the Foundation Project Manager (press **<Alt>** + **<Tab>** to task switch).

3) The design entry is finished.

4) Next you need to implement the design the same way as in the Quick Start OR-Gate lab.

5) Click on the Implementation icon in the Project Manager window and follow the same procedure as in previous labs.

Activity Sheet Experiment 20
4-to-16 Demultiplexer Lab

Name: _____

Date: _____

Using the Simulator

Step 1 :
To simulate the operation of the demultiplexer, first click on the SIM icon in the menu bar at the top of the schematic screen. The Logic Simulator will open.

Step 2:
Next, click on Signal -> Add Signals in the menu bar at the top of the simulator screen. Here you can decide which signals to drive and observe during the simulation. Note that the signals available are A, D, C ,D, and G as well as the outputs: Y15:0 (from the schematic) and something called SimGlobalReset. Recall that what SimGlobalReset does is to simulate a global reset on the PLD. It is always a good idea to use this initially just to ensure that you have a totally reset simulation before you start to drive signals.
Double-click on all of the signals (there will be a red checkmark to indicate selection). Then click on CLOSE at the bottom of the screen.

Step 3:
Now click on Signals -> Add Stimulators in the menu bar at the top of the simulator screen. A box that looks like a keyboard will open. Click on the signal "A" in the upper-left portion of the screen and then on the "A" on the keyboard (on the screen). Do the same for B, using the letter "B" and so on. Then click on "SimGlobalReset" and then on the keyboard click on "R". We can now drive the inputs and the global reset. Pressing the "R" key will toggle the reset, pressing the "A" key will toggle the "A" input to the demultiplexer, and pressing the "G1" key will enable and disable the outputs.

Step 4:
Toggle the "R" and the input signals and then click on the "footsteps" in the menu bar at the top of the screen. Verify that the outputs follow the truth tables in the text.

Step 5:
You can perform a timing simulation of this same design by simply changing the pull-down menu in the menu bar from "Functional" to "Timing".

Now you can physically verify this design by downloading and testing it as in the "Quick Start OR-Gate lab."

Downloading and Testing Your Design

Step 6:
Download the design to the board as in the "Quick Start OR-Gate lab."

Step 7:
To test the design use the switches on the board and observe the LEDs. Refer to your lab book to verify which pins are connected to the switches and LEDs.

Step 8:
Give a brief explanation of how the circuit works.

_____

_____

_____

_____

_____

Experiment 21 Home Security System Lab

Introduction

The purpose of this lab is to build, simulate and download a home security system circuit using the Xilinx Foundation tools and Digilab SpartanXL board.

Objectives

After completing this lab, students will be able to:
- Demonstrate the operation of the circuit described.
- Perform a simple functional and timing simulation using the integrated simulation tool.

Preliminary Procedure

Follow the same steps as in the "Quick Start OR- Gate lab" to set up the lab board.

Procedure

Create a new design with the Xilinx Foundation Series Schematic and name the design Secure. Consult the pin table for the specific board you are using to determine where to lock the input and output pins.
You want to create a design that looks like this:

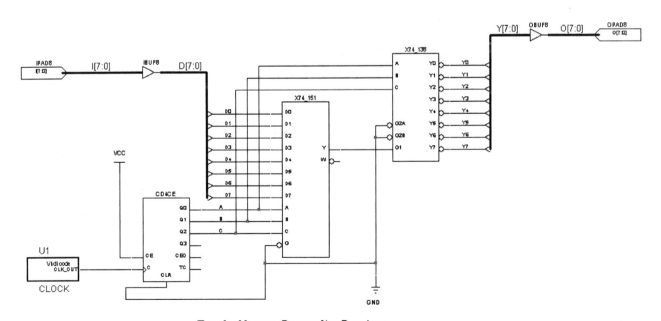

Basic Home Security System

1) To connect two of the symbols to the wires this schematic uses "busses." These are simply a way of drawing several wires as one and saves a lot of time if you need more than 4 wires into a symbol that are all related such as address or data lines. To draw a bus connection, use the Bus icon.

2) Then you have to name the bus such that it has enough names (such as D0, D1, D2, etc.) to satisfy the number of wires that are being represented. You can do this by double-clicking on the bus itself and a window will open that already has the bus range (number of wires) on it and you will have to name it. In this case the output bus was named "O[7:0]. Note that each of the single wires has to have a name such as Y0, Y1, etc. such that the software knows how to route the bus.

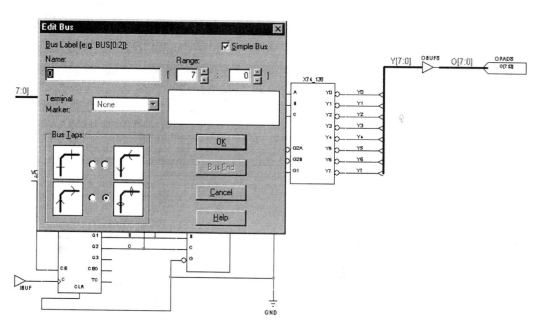

Basic Home Security System

3) As in the previous lab, create macros for inputs called IPAD8 and OPAD8. Use the same procedure as in Experiment 20.

116

4) The clock is instantiated using VHDL code. Your instructor will provide a "black box" OSC4 symbol for you to use, or you may build it yourself. You may recall that we used this same VHDL module in previous labs. This an example of a techniques known as "design re-use". The concept is that you design a module once and can use it in many designs, instead of re-designing it each time you need to use it. Here is the VHDL code for the OSC4 module:

```vhdl
library IEEE;
use IEEE.std_logic_1164.all;
use IEEE.std_logic_unsigned.all;

entity clock is
   port (
      clk_out: inout STD_LOGIC
   );
end clock;

architecture rtl of clock is
   component OSC4 is
      port (
         F8M: out STD_LOGIC;
         F500K: out STD_LOGIC;
         F16K: out STD_LOGIC;
         F490: out STD_LOGIC;
         F15: out STD_LOGIC
      );
   end component;

   component BUFG is
      port (
         I: in STD_LOGIC;
         O: out STD_LOGIC
      );
   end component;

   constant tune: STD_LOGIC_VECTOR(3 downto 0) := "0110";
   signal osc4_clk: STD_LOGIC;
   signal int_clk: STD_LOGIC;
   signal int_clk_out: STD_LOGIC;
begin
   spartan_osc4: OSC4
      port map (F15 => osc4_clk);

   bufg_1: BUFG
      port map (osc4_clk, int_clk);
```

```
clock_divide: process(int_clk)
    variable count: STD_LOGIC_VECTOR(3 downto 0);
begin
    if rising_edge(int_clk) then
        if (count = tune) then
            count := "0000";
            int_clk_out <= not int_clk_out;
        else
            count := count + 1;
        end if;
    end if;
end process clock_divide;

bufg_2: BUFG
    port map (int_clk_out, clk_out);
end rtl;
```

5) Once you finish creating the desired schematic, make sure to save it. <u>Click</u> **File → Save**. Then return to the Foundation Project Manager (press **<Alt>** + **<Tab>** to task switch).

6) The design entry is finished.

7) Next you need to implement the design the same way as in the Quick Start OR-Gate lab.

8) Click on the Implementation icon in the Project Manager window and follow the same procedure as in previous labs.

Activity Sheet Experiment 21
Home Security System Lab

Name: _____

Date: _____

Using the Simulator

Step 1:
To simulate the operation of the home security system, first click on the SIM icon in the menu bar at the top of the schematic screen. The Logic Simulator will open.

Step 2:
Next, click on Signal -> Add Signals in the menu bar at the top of the simulator screen. Here you can decide which signals to drive and observe during the simulation. Note that the signals available are the input bus I[7:0] and CLK, as well as the outputs: O[7:0] (from the schematic) and something called SimGlobalReset. Recall that what SimGlobalReset does is to simulate a global reset on the PLD. It is always a good idea to use this initially just to ensure that you have a totally reset simulation before you start to drive signals.
Double-click on all of the signals (there will be a red checkmark to indicate selection). Then click on CLOSE at the bottom of the screen.

Step 3:
Now click on Signals -> Add Stimulators in the menu bar at the top of the simulator screen. A box that looks like a keyboard will open. Click on the signal "I" in the upper-left portion of the screen and then on the "I" on the keyboard (on the screen). Do the same for CLK using the Bc: line B0 . Then click on "SimGlobalReset" and then on the keyboard click on "R". We can now drive the inputs and the global reset. Pressing the "R" key will toggle the reset and pressing the "I" key will toggle the input bus. Note that the "I" key will toggle all seven inputs from 00 to FF. To be able to individually toggle the signals, right-click on I7 and click on Bus>flatten. Then you can select seven different keyboard letters to drive each input separately.

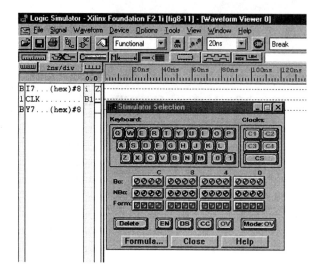

Step 4:
Toggle the "R" and the input signals and then click on the "footsteps" in the menu bar at the top of the screen. Verify that the outputs follow the truth table in the text.

Step 5:
You can perform a timing simulation of this same design by simply changing the pull-down menu in the menu bar from "Functional" to "Timing".

Now you can physically verify this design by downloading and testing it as in the "Quick Start OR-Gate lab."

Downloading and Testing Your Design

Step 6:
Download the design to the board as in the "Quick Start OR-Gate lab."

Step 7:
To test the design, use the switches on the board and observe the LEDs. Refer to your lab book to verify which pins are connected to the switches and LEDs.

Step 8:
Explain in your own words what function the CD4CE component provides in the circuit.

_____

_____

_____

_____

_____

Step 9:
Give a brief explanation of how the circuit works.

_____

_____

_____

_____

_____

Experiment 22 Comparator Lab

Introduction

The purpose of this lab is to build, simulate and download a comparator circuit to control a photocopier using the Xilinx Foundation tools and Digilab SpartanXL board.

Objectives

After completing this lab, students will be able to:
- Demonstrate the operation of the circuit described.
- Perform a simple functional and timing simulation using the integrated simulation tool.

Preliminary Procedure

Follow the same steps as in the "Quick Start OR-Gate lab" to set up the lab board.

Procedure

Create a new design with the Xilinx Foundation Series Schematic and name the design Photoc. Consult the pin table for the specific board you are using to determine where to lock the input and output pins.
You want to create a design that looks like Figure 1:

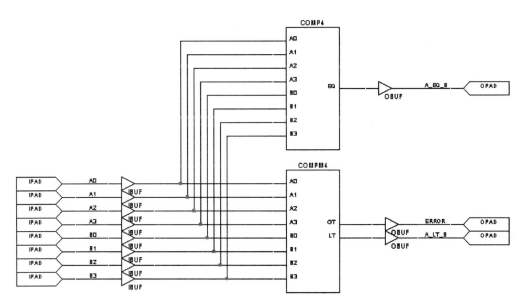

Comparator Control of a Photocopier

Figure 1

1) Once you finish creating the desired schematic, make sure to save it. <u>Click</u> **File → Save**. Then return to the Foundation Project Manager (press **<Alt>** + **<Tab>** to task switch).

2) The design entry is finished.

3) Next you need to implement the design the same way as in the Quick Start OR-Gate lab.

4) Click on the Implementation icon in the Project Manager window and follow the same procedure as in previous labs.

HDL Alternative

Here is the code for the lab in VDHL. Follow the design flow in the "Using Hardware Design Languages (HDLs) with Xilinx tools" tutorial. Don't forget to lock the pins in the ".ucf" file. Here is the VHDL code for the design:

```
library IEEE;
use IEEE.std_logic_1164.all;

entity compare is
   port (
      A: in STD_LOGIC_VECTOR (3 downto 0);
      B: in STD_LOGIC_VECTOR (3 downto 0);
      A_EQ_B: out STD_LOGIC;
      ERROR: out STD_LOGIC;
      A_LT_B: out STD_LOGIC
   );
end compare;

architecture rtl of compare is
begin
   compare: process(A,B)      -- Comparisons are performed in the process
   begin
      if (A < B) then        -- Perform the action below if A < B
         A_EQ_B <= '0';
         ERROR <= '0';
         A_LT_B <= '1';
      elsif (A = B) then     -- Otherwise, if A = B, perform these actions
         A_EQ_B <= '1';
         ERROR <= '0';
         A_LT_B <= '0';
      else                   -- Else do the following actions
         A_EQ_B <= '0';
         ERROR <= '1';
         A_LT_B <= '0';
```

```
        end if;
    end process compare;
end rtl;
```

Here is the same design using Verilog HDL language:

```verilog
module compare (A, B, A_EQ_B, ERROR, A_LT_B) ;
    input [3:0] A;
    input [3:0] B;
    output A_EQ_B;
    output ERROR;
    output A_LT_B;

    reg A_EQ_B;
    reg ERROR;
    reg A_LT_B;

    always @(A or B)  // Run always block when A or B change
        begin: compare
            if (A < B)  // Assign correct outputs when A lt B
                begin
                    A_EQ_B = 1'b 0;
                    A_LT_B = 1'b 1;
                    ERROR = 1'b 0;
                end
            else if (A == B)  // Assign correct outputs when A=B
                begin
                    A_EQ_B = 1'b 1;
                    A_LT_B = 1'b 0;
                    ERROR = 1'b 0;
                end
            else if (A > B)   // Assign correct outputs when A gt B
                begin
                    A_EQ_B = 1'b 0;
                    A_LT_B = 1'b 0;
                    ERROR = 1'b 1;
                end
            else
                begin
                    A_EQ_B = 1'b x;
                    A_LT_B = 1'b x;
                    ERROR = 1'b x;
                end
        end
endmodule
```

Activity Sheet Experiment 22
Comparator Lab

Name: _____

Date: _____

Using the Simulator

Step 1:
To simulate the operation of the comparator, first click on the SIM icon in the menu bar at the top of the schematic screen. The Logic Simulator will open.

Step 2:
Next, click on Signal -> Add Signals in the menu bar at the top of the simulator screen. Here you can decide which signals to drive and observe during the simulation. Note that the signals available are A0-A3, B0-B3, as well as three outputs: A>B, A=B, and A<B (from the schematic), and something called SimGlobalReset. Recall that what SimGlobalReset does is to simulate a global reset on the PLD. It is always a good idea to use this initially just to ensure that you have a totally reset simulation before you start to drive signals.
Double click on all of the signals (there will be a red checkmark to indicate selection). Then click on CLOSE at the bottom of the screen.

Step 3:
Now click on Signals -> Add Stimulators in the menu bar at the top of the simulator screen. A box that looks like a keyboard will open. Click on the signal "A0" in the upper-left portion of the screen and then on the "A" on the keyboard (on the screen). Do the same for A1, using the letter "S", and so on. Then click on "SimGlobalReset" and then on the keyboard click on "R". We can now drive the inputs and the global reset. Pressing the "R" key will toggle the reset and pressing the "A" key will toggle the "A0" input to the comparator and pressing the "S" key will toggle the A1 input.

Step 4:
Toggle the "R" and the input signals and then click on the "footsteps" in the menu bar at the top of the screen. Verify that the outputs follow the truth tables in the text.

Step 5:
You can perform a timing simulation of this same design by simply changing the pull-down menu in the menu bar from "Functional" to "Timing".

Now you can physically verify this design by downloading and testing it as in the "Quick Start OR-Gate lab."

Downloading and Testing Your Design

Step 6:
Download the design to the board as in the "Quick Start OR-Gate lab."

Step 7:
To test the comparator design, use the switches on the board and observe the LEDs. Refer to your lab book to verify which pins are connected to the switches and LEDs.

Step 8:
Give a brief explanation of how the circuit works.

_____

_____

_____

_____

_____

Experiment 23 Parity Generator/Detector Lab

Introduction

The purpose of this lab is to build, simulate, and download a parity generator/detector circuit using the Xilinx Foundation tools and Digilab SpartanXL board.

Objectives

After completing this lab, students will be able to:
- Demonstrate the operation of the circuit described.
- Perform a simple functional and timing simulation using the integrated simulation tool.

Preliminary Procedure

Follow the same steps as in the "Quick Start OR-Gate lab" to set up the lab board.

Procedure

Create a new design with the Xilinx Foundation Series Schematic and name the design Parity. Consult the pin table for the specific board you are using to determine where to lock the input and output pins.
You want to create a design that looks like Figure 1:

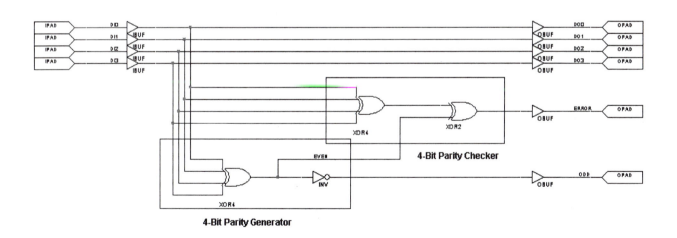

4 Bit Transmission System with Even-Parity

Figure 1

1) Once you finish creating the desired schematic, make sure to save it. <u>Click</u> **File → Save**. Then return to the Foundation Project Manager (press **<Alt>** + **<Tab>** to task switch).

2) The design entry is finished.

3) Next you need to implement the design the same way as in the Quick Start OR-Gate lab.

4) Click on the Implementation icon in the Project Manager window and follow the same procedure as in previous labs.

Activity Sheet Experiment 23
Comparator Lab

Name: _____

Date: _____

Using the Simulator

Step 1:
To simulate the operation of the parity generator/detector, first click on the SIM icon in the menu bar at the top of the schematic screen. The Logic Simulator will open.

Step 2:
Next, click on Signal -> Add Signals in the menu bar at the top of the simulator screen. Here you can decide which signals to drive and observe during the simulation. Note that the signals available are DI0-DI3, as well as the outputs: DO0-DO3, ODD, and ERROR (from the schematic), and something called SimGlobalReset. Recall that what SimGlobalReset does is to simulate a global reset on the PLD. It is always a good idea to use this initially just to ensure that you have a totally reset simulation before you start to drive signals. Double-click on all of the signals (there will be a red checkmark to indicate selection). Then click on CLOSE at the bottom of the screen.

Step 3:
Now click on Signals -> Add Stimulators in the menu bar at the top of the simulator screen. A box that looks like a keyboard will open. Click on the signal "DI0" in the upper-left portion of the screen and then on the "A" on the keyboard (on the screen). Do the same for DI1, using the letter "S" and so on. Then click on "SimGlobalReset" and then on the keyboard click on "R". We can now drive the inputs and the global reset. Pressing the "R" key will toggle the reset, pressing the "A" key will toggle the "DI0" input to the parity generator/detector, and pressing the "S" key will toggle the DI1 input.

Step 4:
Toggle the "R" and the input signals and then click on the "footsteps" in the menu bar at the top of the screen. Verify that the outputs follow the truth tables in the text.

Step 5:
You can perform a timing simulation of this same design by simply changing the pull-down menu in the menu bar from "Functional" to "Timing".

Now you can physically verify this design by locking the pins, recompiling, and downloading and testing it as in the "Quick Start OR-Gate lab."

Downloading and Testing Your Design

Step 6:
Download the design to the board as in the "Quick Start OR-Gate lab."

Step 7:
To test the design, use the switches on the board and observe the LEDs. Refer to your lab book to verify which pins are connected to the switches and LEDs.

Step 8:
Give a brief explanation of how the circuit works.

_____

_____

_____

_____

_____

Experiment 24 S-R Flip-Flop Lab

Introduction

The purpose of this lab is to build, simulate, and download an S-R flip-flop using the Xilinx Foundation tools and Digilab SpartanXL board.

Objectives

After completing this lab, students will be able to:
- Demonstrate the operation of the circuit described.
- Perform a simple functional and timing simulation using the integrated simulation tool.

Preliminary Procedure

Follow the same steps as in the "Quick Start OR-Gate lab" to set up the lab board.

Procedure

Create a new design with the Xilinx Foundation Series Schematic and name the design FLOPS. Consult the pin table for the specific board you are using to determine where to lock the input and output pins.
You want to create a design that looks like this:

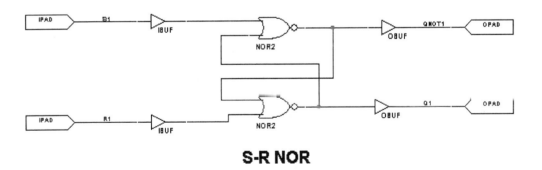

S-R NOR

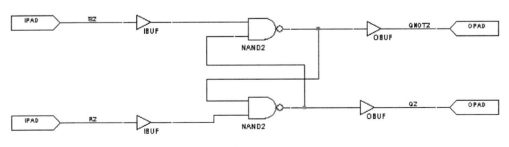

S-R NAND

1) Once you finish creating the desired schematic, make sure to save it. <u>Click</u> **File → Save**. Then return to the Foundation Project Manager (press **<Alt>** + **<Tab>** to task switch).

2) The design entry is finished.

3) Next you need to implement the design the same way as in the Quick Start OR-Gate lab.

4) Click on the Implementation icon in the Project Manager window and follow the same procedure as in previous labs.

Activity Sheet Experiment 24
S-R Flip-Flop Lab

Name: _____

Date: _____

Using the Simulator

Step 1:
To simulate the operation of the S-R flip-flops, first click on the SIM icon in the menu bar at the top of the schematic screen. The Logic Simulator will open.

Step 2:
Next, click on Signal -> Add Signals in the menu bar at the top of the simulator screen. Here you can decide which signals to drive and observe during the simulation. Note that the signals available are S1, R1, S2, and R2, as well as the outputs: Qnot1, Q1, Qnot2, and Q2 (from the schematic), and something called SimGlobalReset. Recall that what SimGlobalReset does is to simulate a global reset on the PLD. It is always a good idea to use this initially just to ensure that you have a totally reset simulation before you start to drive signals.
Double-click on all of the signals (there will be a red checkmark to indicate selection). Then click on CLOSE at the bottom of the screen.

Step 3:
Now click on Signals -> Add Stimulators in the menu bar at the top of the simulator screen. A box that looks like a keyboard will open. Click on the signal "S1" in the upper-left portion of the screen and then on the "S" on the keyboard (on the screen). Do the same for S1, using the letter "D". Choose letters to represent R0 and R1 as well. Then click on "SimGlobalReset" and then on the keyboard click on "R". We can now drive the inputs and the global reset. Pressing the "R" key will toggle the reset and pressing the "S" key will toggle the "S1" input to the S-R NOR flop and pressing the "D" key will toggle the S2 input to the S-R NAND flop.

Step 4:
Toggle the "R" and the input signals and then click on the "footsteps" in the menu bar at the top of the screen. Verify that the outputs follow the truth tables in the text.

Step 5:
You can perform a timing simulation of this same design by simply changing the pull-down menu in the menu bar from "Functional" to "Timing".

Now you can physically verify this design by downloading and testing it as in the "Quick Start OR-Gate lab."

Downloading and Testing Your Design

Step 6:
Download the design to the board as in the "Quick Start OR-Gate lab."

Step 7:
To test the S-R flip-flop design, use the switches on the board and observe the LEDs. Refer to your lab book and schematic to verify which pins are connected to the switches and LEDs.

Step 8:
Give a brief explanation of how an S-R NAND flip-flop is different from an S-R NOR flip-flop.

_____

_____

_____

_____

_____

Step 9:
Give a brief explanation of how the circuits work.

_____

_____

_____

_____

Experiment 25 Master-Slave S-R Flip-Flop Lab

Introduction

The purpose of this lab is to build, simulate, and download a master-slave S-R circuit using the Xilinx Foundation tools and Digilab SpartanXL board.

Objectives

After completing this lab, students will be able to:
- Demonstrate the operation of the circuit described.
- Perform a simple functional and timing simulation using the integrated simulation tool.

Preliminary Procedure

Follow the same steps as in the "Quick Start OR-Gate lab" to set up the lab board.

Procedure

Create a new design with the Xilinx Foundation Series Schematic and name the design Master. Consult the pin table for the specific board you are using to determine where to lock the input and output pins.
You want to create a design that looks like Figure 1:

Figure 1

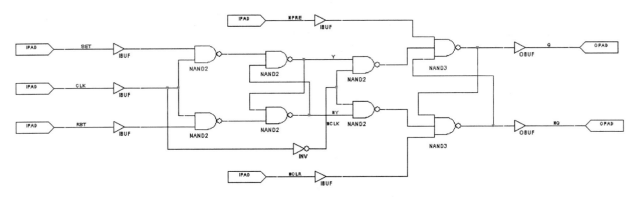

Master-Slave S-R Flip-Flop

1) Once you finish creating the desired schematic, make sure to save it. <u>Click</u> **File → Save**. Then return to the Foundation Project Manager (press **<Alt>** + **<Tab>** to task switch).

2) The design entry is finished.

3) Next you need to implement the design the same way as in the Quick Start OR-Gate lab.

4) Click on the Implementation icon in the Project Manager window and follow the same procedure as in previous labs.

Activity Sheet Experiment 25
Master-Slave S-R Flip-Flop Lab

Name: _____

Date: _____

Using the Simulator

Step 1:
To simulate the operation of the master-slave S-R flip-flops, first click on the SIM icon in the menu bar at the top of the schematic screen. The Logic Simulator will open.

Step 2:
Next, click on Signal -> Add Signals in the menu bar at the top of the simulator screen. Here you can decide which signals to drive and observe during the simulation. Note that the signals available are SET, CLK, RST, NPRE, and NCLR, as well as the outputs: Q and QN (from the schematic), and something called SimGlobalReset. Recall that what SimGlobalReset does is to simulate a global reset on the PLD. It is always a good idea to use this initially just to ensure that you have a totally reset simulation before you start to drive signals.
Double-click on all of the signals (there will be a red checkmark to indicate selection). Then click on CLOSE at the bottom of the screen.

Step 3:
Now click on Signals -> Add Stimulators in the menu bar at the top of the simulator screen. A box that looks like a keyboard will open. Click on the signal "SET" in the upper-left portion of the screen and then on the "S" on the keyboard (on the screen). Do the same for RST, using the letter "D". Choose letters to represent RST, NPRE, and NCLR as well. Then click on "SimGlobalReset" and then on the keyboard click on "R". Drive the Clock as in previous labs using the Bc: line on the dialog box.
We can now drive the inputs and the global reset. Pressing the "R" key will toggle the global reset and pressing the "D" key will toggle the "RST" input to the Master-Slave circuit. Similarly, pressing the "S" key will toggle the "SET" input.

Step 4:
Toggle the "R" and the input signals and then click on the "footsteps" in the menu bar at the top of the screen. Verify that the outputs follow the truth tables in the text.

Step 5:
You can perform a timing simulation of this same design by simply changing the pull-down menu in the menu bar from "Functional" to "Timing". Note: Due to the way the simulator functions, this circuit will probably ONLY work using a timing simulation.

Now you can physically verify this design by downloading and testing it as in the "Quick Start OR-Gate lab."

Downloading and Testing Your Design

Step 6:
Download the design to the board as in the "Quick Start OR-Gate lab."

Step 7:
To test the master-slave S-R flip-flop design, use the switches on the board and observe the LEDs. Refer to your lab book to verify which pins are connected to the switches and LEDs.

Step 8:
Give a brief explanation of the function of the first and third sets of NAND gates (looking from left to right), in the circuit of Figure 1.

_____

_____

_____

_____

_____

Step 9:
Give a brief explanation of how the circuit works.

_____

_____

_____

_____

_____

Experiment 26 D Flip-Flop Lab

Introduction

The purpose of this lab is to build, simulate, and download a D flip-flop using the Xilinx Foundation tools and Digilab SpartanXL board.

Objectives

After completing this lab, students will be able to:
- Demonstrate the operation of the circuit described.
- Perform a simple functional and timing simulation using the integrated simulation tool.

Preliminary Procedure

Follow the same steps as in the "Quick Start OR-Gate lab" to set up the lab board.

Procedure

Create a new design with the Xilinx Foundation Series Schematic and name the design DFLOP. Consult the pin table for the specific board you are using to determine where to lock the input and output pins.
You want to create a design that looks like Figure 1:

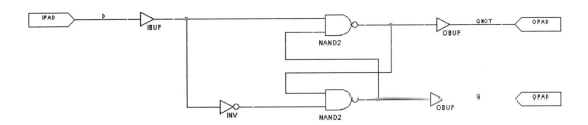

Basic D Flip-Flop

Figure 1

1) Once you finish creating the desired schematic, make sure to save it. <u>Click</u> **File → Save**. Then return to the Foundation Project Manager (press **<Alt>** + **<Tab>** to task switch).

2) The design entry is finished.

3) Next you need to implement the design the same way as in the Quick Start OR-Gate lab.

4) Click on the Implementation icon in the Project Manager window and follow the same procedure as in previous labs.

Activity Sheet Experiment 26
D Flip-Flop Lab

Name: _____

Date: _____

Using the Simulator

Step 1:
To simulate the operation of the D flops, first click on the SIM icon in the menu bar at the top of the schematic screen. The Logic Simulator will open.

Step 2:
Next, click on Signal -> Add Signals in the menu bar at the top of the simulator screen. Here you can decide which signals to drive and observe during the simulation. Note that the signals available are D, as well as the outputs: Qnot and Q (from the schematic), and something called SimGlobalReset. Recall that what SimGlobalReset does is to simulate a global reset on the PLD. It is always a good idea to use this initially just to ensure that you have a totally reset simulation before you start to drive signals.
Double-click on all of the signals (there will be a red checkmark to indicate selection). Then click on CLOSE at the bottom of the screen.

Step 3:
Now click on Signals -> Add Stimulators in the menu bar at the top of the simulator screen. A box that looks like a keyboard will open. Click on the signal "D" in the upper-left portion of the screen and then on the "D" on the keyboard (on the screen). Choose letters to represent QNOT and Q as well. Then click on "SimGlobalReset" and then on the keyboard click on "R". We can now drive the inputs and the global reset. Pressing the "R" key will toggle the reset, and pressing the "D" key will toggle the "D" input to the D flop.

Step 4:
Toggle the "R" and the input signals and then click on the "footsteps" in the menu bar at the top of the screen. Verify that the outputs follow the truth tables in the text.

Step 5:
You can perform a timing simulation of this same design by simply changing the pull-down menu in the menu bar from "Functional" to "Timing".

Now you can physically verify this design by downloading and testing it as in the "Quick Start OR-Gate lab."

Downloading and Testing Your Design

Step 6:
Download the design to the board as in the "Quick Start OR-Gate lab."

Step 7:
To test the D flip-flop design, use the switches on the board and observe the LEDs. Refer to your lab book to verify which pins are connected to the switches and LEDs.

Step 8:
Give a brief explanation of how the circuit works.

_____

_____

_____

_____

_____

Experiment 27
Divide-by-Two Counter and Storage Register Lab

Introduction

The purpose of this lab is to build, simulate and download two circuits: A divide-by-two counter and a storage register circuit using the Xilinx Foundation tools and Digilab SpartanXL board. This demonstrates how different functions – related or unrelated – can be designed into a single PLD.

Objectives

After completing this lab, students will be able to:
- Demonstrate the operation of the circuits described.
- Perform a simple functional and timing simulation using the integrated simulation tool.

Preliminary Procedure

Follow the same steps as in the "Quick Start OR-Gate lab" to set up the lab board.

Procedure

Create a new design with the Xilinx Foundation Series Schematic and name the design Div2. Consult the pin table for the specific board you are using to determine where to lock the input and output pins.
You want to create a design that looks like Figure 1:

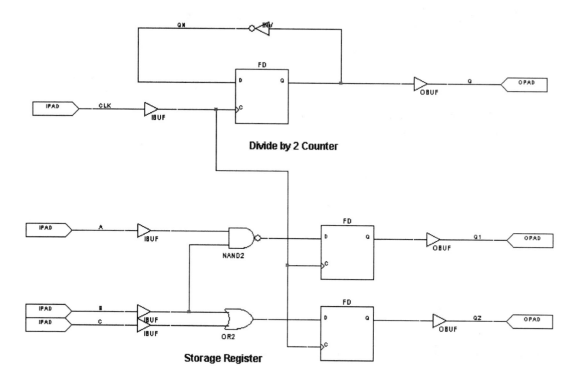

Divide by 2 Counter

Storage Register

D Flip-Flop Applications

Figure 1

1) Once you finish creating the desired schematic, make sure to save it. <u>Click</u> **File → Save**. Then return to the Foundation Project Manager (press **<Alt>** + **<Tab>** to task switch).

2) The design entry is finished.

3) Next you need to implement the design the same way as in the Quick Start OR-Gate lab.

4) Click on the Implementation icon in the Project Manager window and follow the same procedure as in previous labs.

Activity Sheet Experiment 27
Divide-by-Two Counter and Storage Register Lab

Name: _____

Date: _____

Using the Simulator

Step 1:
To simulate the operation of the circuits, first click on the SIM icon in the menu bar at the top of the schematic screen. The Logic Simulator will open.

Step 2:
Next, click on Signal -> Add Signals in the menu bar at the top of the simulator screen. Here you can decide which signals to drive and observe during the simulation. Note that the signals available are A, B, C, and CLK, as well as the outputs: Q, Q1, and Q2 (from the schematic), and SimGlobalReset. Recall that what SimGlobalReset does is to simulate a global reset on the PLD. It is always a good idea to use this initially just to ensure that you have a totally reset simulation before you start to drive signals.
Double-click on all of the signals (there will be a red checkmark to indicate selection). Then click on CLOSE at the bottom of the screen.

Step 3:
Now click on Signals -> Add Stimulators in the menu bar at the top of the simulator screen. A box that looks like a keyboard will open. Click on the signal "A" in the upper left portion of the screen and then on the "A" on the keyboard (on the screen). Do the same for B, using the letter "B". Again do the same thing for "C" using the letter "C". To stimulate the clock, select the CLK signal from the list and then click on the "B0" button below the "0" in the stimulus dialog box as shown below. Then click on "SimGlobalReset" and then on the keyboard click on "R". We can now drive the inputs and the global reset. Pressing the "R" key will toggle the reset and pressing the "A" key will toggle the "A" input to the Storage register flip-flop, and so on.

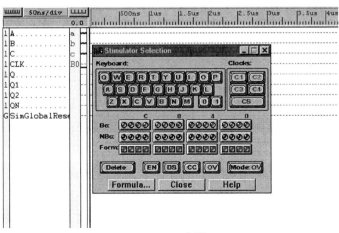

147

Step 4:

Toggle the "R" and the input signals and then click on the "footsteps" in the menu bar at the top of the screen. Verify that the outputs follow the truth tables in the text.

Step 5:

You can perform a timing simulation of this same design by simply changing the pull-down menu in the menu bar from "Functional" to "Timing".

Now you can physically verify this design by downloading and testing it as in the "Quick Start OR-Gate lab."

Downloading and Testing Your Design

Step 6: Download the design to the board as in the "Quick Start OR-Gate lab."

Step 7:

To test the divide-by-two and storage register design, use the switches on the board and observe the LEDs. Refer to your lab book to verify which pins are connected to the switches and LEDs.

Step 8:

Give a brief explanation of the function of the FD component with the output inverted and fed back to the input.

_____

_____

_____

_____

_____

Step 9:

Give a brief explanation of how the circuit works.

_____

_____

_____

_____

_____

Experiment 28 Edge-Triggered J-K Flip-Flop Lab

Introduction

The purpose of this lab is to build, simulate, and download an edge-triggered J-K flip-flop circuit using the Xilinx Foundation tools and Digilab SpartanXL board. This demonstrates how different functions – related or unrelated – can be designed into a single PLD.

Objectives

After completing this lab, students will be able to:
- Demonstrate the operation of the circuit described.
- Perform a simple functional and timing simulation using the integrated simulation tool.

Preliminary Procedure

Follow the same steps as in the "Quick Start OR-Gate lab" to set up the lab board.

Procedure

Create a new design with the Xilinx Foundation Series Schematic and name the design EJK. Consult the pin table for the specific board you are using to determine where to lock the input and output pins.
You want to create a design that looks like Figure 1:

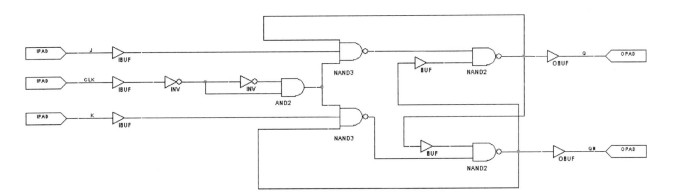

Edge-Triggered J-K Flip-FLops
Figure 1

1) Once you finish creating the desired schematic, make sure to save it. Click **File → Save**. Then return to the Foundation Project Manager (press **<Alt>** + **<Tab>** to task switch).

2) The design entry is finished.

3) Next, you need to implement the design the same way as in the Quick Start OR-Gate lab.

4) Click on the Implementation icon in the Project Manager window and follow the same procedure as in previous labs.

Activity Sheet Experiment 28
Edge-Triggered J-K Flip-Flop Lab

Name: _____

Date: _____

Using the Simulator

Step 1:
To simulate the operation of the circuits, first click on the SIM icon in the menu bar at the top of the schematic screen. The Logic Simulator will open.

Step 2:
Next, click on Signal -> Add Signals in the menu bar at the top of the simulator screen. Here you can decide which signals to drive and observe during the simulation. Note that the signals available are J, K, and CLK, as well as the outputs: Q and QN (from the schematic), and SimGlobalReset. Recall that what SimGlobalReset does is to simulate a global reset on the PLD. It is always a good idea to use this initially just to ensure that you have a totally reset simulation before you start to drive signals.
Double-click on all of the signals (there will be a red checkmark to indicate selection). Then click on CLOSE at the bottom of the screen.

Step 3:
Now click on Signals -> Add Stimulators in the menu bar at the top of the simulator screen. A box that looks like a keyboard will open. Click on the signal "J" in the upper-left portion of the screen and then on the "J" on the keyboard (on the screen). Do the same for K, using the letter "K".
To stimulate the clock, select the CLK signal from the list and then click on the "B$_C$: 0" button below the "0" in the stimulus dialog box as shown below. Then click on "SimGlobalReset" and then on the keyboard click on "R". We can now drive the inputs and the global reset. Pressing the "R" key will toggle the reset and pressing the "J" key will toggle the "J" input to the flip-flop, and so on.

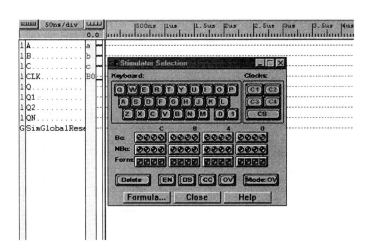

Step 4:
Toggle the "R" and the input signals and then click on the "footsteps" in the menu bar at the top of the screen. Verify that the outputs follow the truth tables in the text.

Step 5:
You can perform a timing simulation of this same design by simply changing the pull-down menu in the menu bar from "Functional" to "Timing". Note: This simulation will probably only work in Timing mode due to the way the simulator works. Why is that?

Now you can physically verify this design by downloading and testing it as in the "Quick Start OR-Gate lab."

Downloading and Testing Your Design

Step 6:
Download the design to the board as in the "Quick Start OR-Gate lab."

Step 7:
To test the design, use the switches on the board and observe the LEDs. Refer to your lab book to verify which pins are connected to the switches and LEDs.

Step 8:
Give a brief explanation of the function of the AND2 component in this circuit.

_____

_____

_____

_____

_____

Step 9:
Give a brief explanation of how the circuit works.

_____

_____

_____

_____

_____

Experiment 29 4-Bit Binary Counter Lab

Introduction

The purpose of this lab is to build, simulate, and download a 4-bit binary counter circuit using the Xilinx Foundation tools and Digilab SpartanXL board. This demonstrates how different functions – related or unrelated – can be designed into a single PLD.

Objectives

After completing this lab, students will be able to:
- Demonstrate the operation of the circuit described.
- Perform a simple functional and timing simulation using the integrated simulation tool.

Preliminary Procedure

Follow the same steps as in the "Quick Start OR-Gate lab" to set up the lab board.

Procedure

Create a new design with the Xilinx Foundation Series Schematic and name the design BC4. Consult the pin table for the specific board you are using to determine where to lock the input and output pins.

You want to create a design that looks like the schematic below:

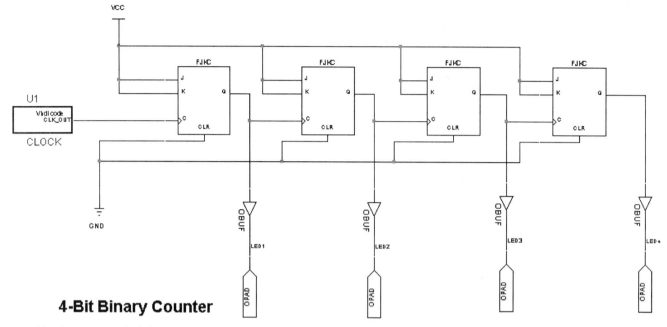

4-Bit Binary Counter

1) Once you finish creating the desired schematic, make sure to save it. <u>Click</u> **File → Save**. Then return to the Foundation Project Manager (press **<Alt>** + **<Tab>** to task switch).

2) The design entry is finished.

3) Next you need to implement the design the same way as in the Quick Start OR-Gate lab.

4) Click on the Implementation icon in the Project Manager window and follow the same procedure as in previous labs.

5) Note that this lab also uses the VHDL code version of the OCS4 symbol as used in previous experiments.

HDL Alternative

Here is the code for the lab in VDHL. Follow the design flow in the "Using Hardware Design Languages (HDLs) with Xilinx tools" tutorial. Don't forget to lock the pins in the ".ucf" file.

Here is the VHDL code for the 3-bit counter in this design:

library IEEE;
use IEEE.std_logic_1164.all;
use IEEE.std_logic_unsigned.all;   -- Used for addition operator

```vhdl
entity bc4 is
  port (
    LED: inout STD_LOGIC_VECTOR (3 downto 0) -- LED declared as both input
  );                                          -- and output
end bc4;

architecture rtl of bc4 is
  component clock                    -- Internal clock generator
    port (                           -- component
      clk_out: inout STD_LOGIC
    );
  end component;

  signal clk: STD_LOGIC;
begin
  generate_clock: clock
    port map (clk);

  counter: process(clk)
  begin
    if rising_edge(clk) then         -- On the rising edge of clk
        if (LED = "1111") then           -- Reset to 0 if LED is at max
        LED <= "0000";
      else
        LED <= LED + "0001";         -- Otherwise increment by one
      end if;
    end if;
  end process counter;
end rtl;
```

Note that you also need to use the VHDL code for the "OSC4" as in previous experiments.

Here is the same design using the Verilog HDL:

```verilog
module compare (A, B, A_EQ_B, ERROR, A_LT_B) ;
  input [3:0] A;
  input [3:0] B;
  output A_EQ_B;
  output ERROR;
  output A_LT_B;

  reg A_EQ_B;
  reg ERROR;
  reg A_LT_B;
```

```verilog
always @(A or B)  // Run always block when A or B change
   begin: compare
      if (A < B)  // Assign correct outputs when A lt B
        begin
           A_EQ_B = 1'b 0;
           A_LT_B = 1'b 1;
           ERROR = 1'b 0;
        end
      else if (A == B)  // Assign correct outputs when A=B
        begin
           A_EQ_B = 1'b 1;
           A_LT_B = 1'b 0;
           ERROR = 1'b 0;
        end
      else if (A > B)   // Assign correct outputs when A gt B
        begin
           A_EQ_B = 1'b 0;
           A_LT_B = 1'b 0;
           ERROR = 1'b 1;
        end
      else
        begin
           A_EQ_B = 1'b x;
           A_LT_B = 1'b x;
           ERROR = 1'b x;
        end
   end
endmodule
```

Activity Sheet Experiment 29
4-Bit Binary Counter Lab

Name: _____

Date: _____

Using the Simulator

Step 1:
To simulate the operation of the circuits, first click on the SIM icon in the menu bar at the top of the schematic screen. The Logic Simulator will open.

Step 2:
Next, click on Signal -> Add Signals in the menu bar at the top of the simulator screen. Here you can decide which signals to drive and observe during the simulation. Note that the signals available are CLK, as well as the outputs: LED1-LED4 (from the schematic), and SimGlobalReset. Recall that what SimGlobalReset does is to simulate a global reset on the PLD. It is always a good idea to use this initially just to ensure that you have a totally reset simulation before you start to drive signals.
Double-click on all of the signals (there will be a red checkmark to indicate selection). Then click on CLOSE at the bottom of the screen.

Step 3:
Now click on Signals -> Add Stimulators in the menu bar at the top of the simulator screen. A box that looks like a keyboard will open.
To stimulate the clock, select the CLK signal from the list and then click on the "B_C: 0" button below the "0" in the stimulus dialog box as shown below. Then click on "SimGlobalReset" and then on the keyboard click on "R". We can now drive the CLK and the global reset. Pressing the "R" key will toggle the reset.

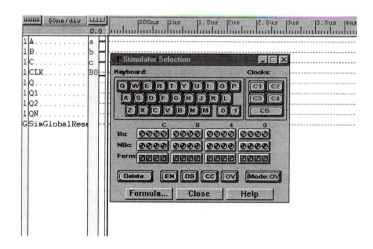

Step 4:
Toggle the "R" and then click on the "footsteps" in the menu bar at the top of the screen. Verify that the outputs follow the truth tables in the text.

Step 5:
You can perform a timing simulation of this same design by simply changing the pull-down menu in the menu bar from "Functional" to "Timing". Note: This simulation will probably only work without glitches in Timing mode due to the way the simulator works. Why is that?

_____

Now you can physically verify this design by downloading and testing it as in the "Quick Start OR-Gate lab."

Downloading and Testing Your Design

Step 6:
Download the design to the board as in the "Quick Start OR-Gate lab."

Step 7:
To test the design, use the switches on the board and observe the LEDs. Refer to your lab book to verify which pins are connected to the switches and LEDs.

Step 8: Give a brief explanation of why you did or did not get glitches in the functional simulation mode when using the simulator.

_____

_____

_____

_____

_____

Step 9: Give a brief explanation of how the circuit works.

_____

_____

_____

_____

Experiment 30 Divide-by-Four Circuit Lab

Introduction

The purpose of this lab is to build, simulate, and download a divide-by-four circuit using the Xilinx Foundation tools and Digilab SpartanXL board. This demonstrates how different functions – related or unrelated – can be designed into a single PLD device.

Objectives

After completing this lab, students will be able to:
- Demonstrate the operation of the circuit described.
- Perform a simple functional and timing simulation using the integrated simulation tool.

Preliminary Procedure

Follow the same steps as in the "Quick Start OR-Gate lab" to set up the lab board.

Procedure

Create a new design with the Xilinx Foundation Series Schematic and name the design Div4. Consult the pin table for the specific board you are using to determine where to lock the input and output pins.
You want to create a design that looks like this:

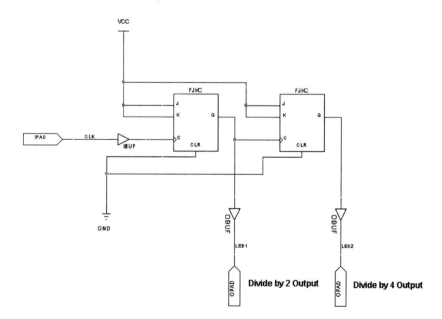

Divide-by-Four Circuit

1) Once you finish creating the desired schematic, make sure to save it. <u>Click</u> **File → Save**. Then return to the Foundation Project Manager (press **<Alt>** + **<Tab>** to task switch).

2) The design entry is finished.

3) Next you need to implement the design the same way as in the Quick Start OR-Gate lab.

4) Click on the Implementation icon in the Project Manager window and follow the same procedure as in previous labs.

Activity Sheet Experiment 30
Divide-by-Four Circuit Lab

Name: _____

Date: _____

Using the Simulator

Step 1:
To simulate the operation of the circuits, first click on the SIM icon in the menu bar at the top of the schematic screen. The Logic Simulator will open.

Step 2:
Next, click on Signal -> Add Signals in the menu bar at the top of the simulator screen. Here you can decide which signals to drive and observe during the simulation. Note that the signals available are CLK, as well as the outputs: LED1 and LED2 (from the schematic), and SimGlobalReset. Recall that what SimGlobalReset does is to simulate a global reset on the PLD. It is always a good idea to use this initially just to ensure that you have a totally reset simulation before you start to drive signals.
Double-click on all of the signals (there will be a red checkmark to indicate selection). Then click on CLOSE at the bottom of the screen.

Step 3:
Now click on Signals -> Add Stimulators in the menu bar at the top of the simulator screen. A box that looks like a keyboard will open.
To stimulate the clock select the CLK signal from the list and then click on the "B_C:0" button below the "0" in the stimulus dialog box as shown below. Then click on "SimGlobalReset" and then on the keyboard click on "R". We can now drive the CLK and the global reset. Pressing the "R" key will toggle the reset.

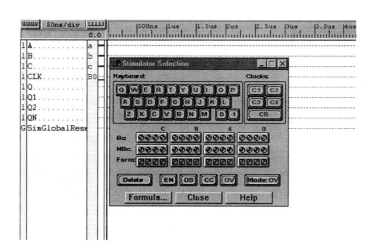

Step 4:

Toggle the "R" and then click on the "footsteps" in the menu bar at the top of the screen. Verify that the outputs follow the truth tables in the text.

Step 5:

You can perform a timing simulation of this same design by simply changing the pull-down menu in the menu bar from "Functional" to "Timing". Note: This simulation will probably only work without glitches in Timing mode due to the way the simulator works. Why is that?

Now you can physically verify this design by downloading and testing it as in the "Quick Start OR-Gate lab."

Downloading and Testing Your Design

Step 6:

Download the design to the board as in the "Quick Start OR-Gate lab."

Step 7:

To test the design, use the switches on the board and observe the LEDs in the LED bar. Refer to your lab book to verify which pins are connected to the switches and LEDs.

Step 8:

Give a brief explanation of why you did or did not get glitches in the functional simulation mode when using the simulator.

_____

_____

_____

_____

Step 9:

Give a brief explanation of how the circuit works.

_____

_____

_____

_____

Experiment 31 One-Shot Emulator Lab

Introduction

The purpose of this lab is to build, simulate and download a one-shot circuit using the Xilinx Foundation tools and Digilab Spartan board. This demonstrates how an analog function can be emulated in a CPLD.

Objectives

After completing this lab, the student will be able to:
- Demonstrate the operation of the circuit described.
- Perform a simple functional and timing simulation using the integrated simulation tool.
- Explain how the counter is emulating a 555 one-shot timer.

Preliminary Procedure

Follow the same steps as in the "Quick Start OR-Gate lab" to set up the lab board.

Procedure

Create a new design with the Xilinx Foundation Series Schematic and name the design Oneshot. Consult the pin table for the specific board you are using to determine where to lock the input and output pins. You want to create a design that looks like this:

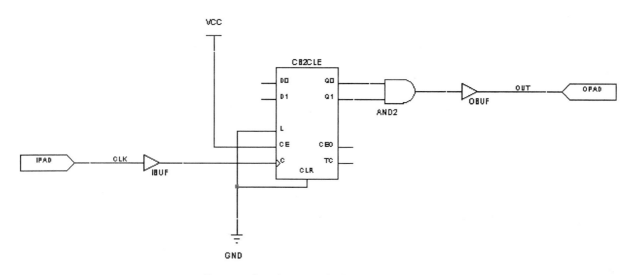

One-shot emulator

1) Once you finish creating the desired schematic, make sure to save it. <u>Click</u> **File → Save**. Then return to the Foundation Project Manager (press **<Alt>** + **<Tab>** to task switch).

2) The design entry is finished.

3) Next you need to implement the design the same way as in the Quick Start OR-Gate lab.

4) Click on the Implementation icon in the Project Manager window and follow the same procedure as in previous labs.

Activity Sheet Experiment 31
One-Shot Emulator Lab

Name: _____

Date: _____

Using the Simulator

Step 1:
To simulate the operation of the circuits, first click on the SIM icon in the menu bar at the top of the schematic screen. The Logic Simulator will open.

Step 2:
Next, click on Signal -> Add Signals in the menu bar at the top of the simulator screen. Here you can decide which signals to drive and observe during the simulation. Note that the signals available are CLK and OUT (from the schematic), and SimGlobalReset. Recall that what SimGlobalReset does is to simulate a global reset on the PLD. It is always a good idea to use this initially just to ensure that you have a totally reset simulation before you start to drive signals.
Double-click on all of the signals (there will be a red checkmark to indicate selection). Then click on CLOSE at the bottom of the screen.

Step 3:
Now click on Signals -> Add Stimulators in the menu bar at the top of the simulator screen. A box that looks like a keyboard will open.
To stimulate the clock, select the CLK signal from the list and then click on the "Bc: 0" button below the "0" in the first row of the stimulus dialog box as shown below. Then click on "SimGlobalReset" and then on the keyboard click on "R". We can now drive the CLK and the global reset. Pressing the "R" key will toggle the reset.

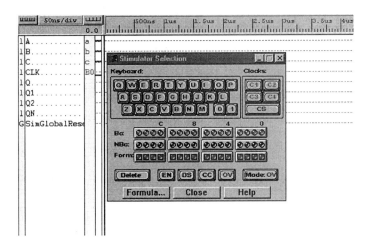

Step 4:

Toggle the "R" and then click on the "footsteps" in the menu bar at the top of the screen. Verify that the outputs follow the truth tables in the text.

Step 5:

You can perform a timing simulation of this same design by simply changing the pull-down menu in the menu bar from "Functional" to "Timing".

Now you can physically verify this design by downloading and testing it as in the "Quick Start OR-Gate lab."

Downloading and Testing Your Design

Step 6:

Download the design to the board as in the "Quick Start OR-Gate lab."

Step 7:

To test the design, use the switches on the board and observe the LEDs. Refer to your lab book to verify which pins are connected to the switches and LEDs.

Step 8:

Give a brief explanation of how this circuit is emulating a 555 timer. How else might you use a counter to emulate the operation of a 555 timer?

_____

_____

_____

_____

_____

Experiment 32 Buffer Register Lab

Introduction

The purpose of this lab is to build, simulate, and download a buffer register circuit using the Xilinx Foundation tools and Digilab Spartan board. This demonstrates how different functions – related or unrelated – can be designed into a single CPLD.

Objectives

After completing this lab, the student will be able to:
- Demonstrate the operation of the circuit described.
- Perform a simple functional and timing simulation using the integrated simulation tool.

Preliminary Procedure

Follow the same steps as in the "Quick Start OR-Gate lab" to set up the lab board.

Procedure

Create a new design with the Xilinx Foundation Series Schematic and name the design Bufreg. Consult the pin table for the specific board you are using to determine where to lock the input and output pins. You want to create a design that looks like Figure 1:

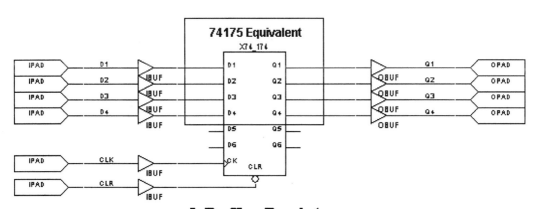

A Buffer Register

Figure 1

1) Once you finish creating the desired schematic, make sure to save it. <u>Click</u> **File → Save**. Then return to the Foundation Project Manager (press **\<Alt>** + **\<Tab>** to task switch).

2) The design entry is finished.

3) Next you need to implement the design the same way as in the Quick Start OR-Gate lab.

4) Click on the Implementation icon in the Project Manager window and follow the same procedure as in previous labs.

HDL Alternative

Here is the code for the lab in VDHL. Follow the design flow in the "Using Hardware Design Languages (HDLs) with Xilinx tools" tutorial. Don't forget to lock the pins in the ".ucf" file.

```
library IEEE;
use IEEE.std_logic_1164.all;

entity bufreg is
    port (
        D: in STD_LOGIC_VECTOR (3 downto 0);
        CLR: in STD_LOGIC;
        CLK: in STD_LOGIC;
        Q: out STD_LOGIC_VECTOR (3 downto 0)
    );
end bufreg;

architecture rtl of bufreg is
begin
    store_data: process(CLK, CLR)
    begin
        if (CLR = '0') then  -- Asynchronous reset when CLR = '1'
            Q <= "0000";
        elsif rising_edge(clk) then  -- Buffer & register the
            Q <= D;                   -- input to the output
        end if;
    end process store_data;
end rtl;
```

Here is the same design using the Verilog HDL:

```verilog
module bufreg (D, CLR, CLK, Q);
    input [3:0] D;
    input CLR;
    input CLK;
    output [3:0] Q;

    reg [3:0] Q;

    always @(posedge CLK or negedge CLR)  // Run on positive
        begin: store_data              // edge of CLK or CLR
            if (!CLR)
                Q = 4'b 0000;  // Assign 0 to output if CLR is high
            else
                Q = D;         // Otherwise assign D to Q (register)
        end
endmodule
```

Activity Sheet Experiment 32
Buffer Register Lab

Name: _____

Date: _____

Using the Simulator

Step 1:
To simulate the operation of the circuits, first click on the SIM icon in the menu bar at the top of the schematic screen. The Logic Simulator will open.

Step 2:
Next, click on Signal -> Add Signals in the menu bar at the top of the simulator screen. Here you can decide which signals to drive and observe during the simulation. Note that the signals available are D1-D4, CLK, and CLR, as well as the outputs: Q1-Q4 (from the schematic), and SimGlobalReset. Recall that what SimGlobalReset does is to simulate a global reset on the PLD. It is always a good idea to use this initially just to ensure that you have a totally reset simulation before you start to drive signals.
Double-click on all of the signals (there will be a red checkmark to indicate selection). Then click on CLOSE at the bottom of the screen.

Step 3:
Now click on Signals -> Add Stimulators in the menu bar at the top of the simulator screen. A box that looks like a keyboard will open. Click on the signal "D1" in the upper-left portion of the screen and then on the "A" on the keyboard (on the screen). Do the same for D2 using the "S" key on the keyboard, and so on .
To stimulate the clock, select the CLK signal from the list and then click on the "B$_C$: 0" button below the "0" in the stimulus dialog box as shown below. Then click on "SimGlobalReset" and then on the keyboard click on "R". We can now drive the CLK and the global reset. Pressing the "R" key will toggle the reset.

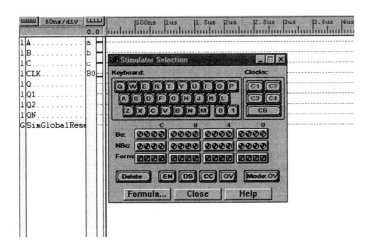

Step 4:

Toggle the "R" and then click on the "footsteps" in the menu bar at the top of the screen. Verify that the outputs follow the truth tables in the text.

Step 5:

You can perform a timing simulation of this same design by simply changing the pull-down menu in the menu bar from "Functional" to "Timing". Now you can physically verify this design by downloading and testing it as in the "Quick Start OR-Gate lab."

Downloading and Testing Your Design

Step 6:

Download the design to the board as in the "Quick Start OR-Gate lab."

Step 7:

To test the design, use the switches on the board and observe the LEDs. Refer to your lab book to verify which pins are connected to the switches and LEDs.

Step 8:

Give a brief explanation of what happens to the unconnected pins when you compile and implement the design.

_____

_____

_____

_____

_____

Step 9:

Give a brief explanation of how the circuit works.

_____

_____

_____

_____

_____

Experiment 33
Serial-In, Serial-Out (SISO) Shift Register Lab

Introduction

The purpose of this lab is to build, simulate and download a SISO register circuit using the Xilinx Foundation tools and Digilab Spartan board. This demonstrates how different functions – related or unrelated – can be designed into a single CPLD.

Objectives

After completing this lab, students will be able to:
- Demonstrate the operation of the circuit described.
- Perform a simple functional and timing simulation using the integrated simulation tool.

Preliminary Procedure

Follow the same steps as in the "Quick Start OR-Gate lab" to set up the lab board.

Procedure

Create a new design with the Xilinx Foundation Series Schematic and name the design SISO. Consult the pin table for the specific board you are using to determine where to lock the input and output pins. You want to create a design that looks like this:

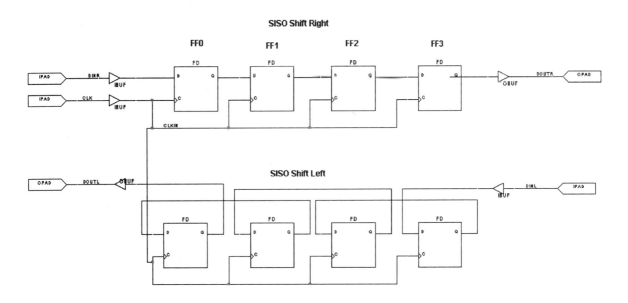

Serial-In Serial-Out Shift Registers (SISO)

1) Once you finish creating the desired schematic, make sure to save it. <u>Click</u> **File → Save**. Then return to the Foundation Project Manager (press **<Alt>** + **<Tab>** to task switch).

2) The design entry is finished.

3) Next you need to implement the design the same way as in the Quick Start OR-Gate lab.

4) Click on the Implementation icon in the Project Manager window and follow the same procedure as in previous labs.

HDL Alternative

Here is the code for the lab in VDHL. Follow the design flow in the "Using Hardware Design Languages (HDLs) with Xilinx tools" tutorial. Don't forget to lock the pins in the ".ucf" file.

```vhdl
library IEEE;
use IEEE.std_logic_1164.all;

entity siso is
   port (
      DINR: in STD_LOGIC;
      DINL: in STD_LOGIC;
      CLK: in STD_LOGIC;
      DOUTR: out STD_LOGIC;
      DOUTL: out STD_LOGIC
   );
end siso;

architecture rtl of siso is
   signal rreg: STD_LOGIC_VECTOR(3 downto 0);
   signal lreg: STD_LOGIC_VECTOR(3 downto 0);
begin
   right_shift_register: process(CLK)
   begin
      if rising_edge(CLK) then
         DOUTR <= rreg(3);
         rreg <= rreg(2 downto 0) & DINR;
      end if;
   end process right_shift_register;

   left_shift_register: process(CLK)
   begin
```

```
      if rising_edge(CLK) then
         DOUTL <= lreg(0);
         lreg <= DINL & lreg(3 downto 1);
      end if;
   end process left_shift_register;
end rtl;
```

Here is the same design using the Verilog HDL:

```
module siso (DINR, DINL, CLK, DOUTR, DOUTL);
   input DINR;
   input DINL;
   input CLK;
   output DOUTR;
   output DOUTL;

   reg DOUTR;
   reg DOUTL;
   reg [3:0] rreg;
   reg [3:0] lreg;

   always @(posedge CLK)
      begin: right_shift_register
         DOUTR = rreg[3];
         rreg = {rreg[2:0], DINR};
      end

   always @(posedge CLK)
      begin: left_shift_register
         DOUTL = lreg[0];
         lreg = {DINL, lreg[3:1]};
      end
endmodule
```

Briefly describe the similarities and differences between the VHDL and Verilog versions of
the design:

_____

_____

_____

_____

Activity Sheet Experiment 33
Serial-In, Serial-Out (SISO) Shift Register Lab

Name: _____

Date: _____

Using the Simulator

Step 1:
To simulate the operation of the circuits, first click on the SIM icon in the menu bar at the top of the schematic screen. The Logic Simulator will open.

Step 2:
Next, click on Signal -> Add Signals in the menu bar at the top of the simulator screen. Here you can decide which signals to drive and observe during the simulation. Note that the signals available are DINR, DINL, and CLK, as well as the outputs: DOUTR and DOUTL (from the schematic), and SimGlobalReset. Recall that what SimGlobalReset does is to simulate a global reset on the PLD. It is always a good idea to use this initially just to ensure that you have a totally reset simulation before you start to drive signals.
Double-click on all of the signals (there will be a red checkmark to indicate selection). Then click on CLOSE at the bottom of the screen.

Step 3:
Now click on Signals -> Add Stimulators in the menu bar at the top of the simulator screen. A box that looks like a keyboard will open Click on the signal "DINR" in the upper left portion of the screen and then on the "A" on the keyboard (on the screen). Do the same for DINL using the "S" key on the keyboard .
To stimulate the clock, select the CLK signal from the list and then click on the "Bc: 0" button below the "0" in the stimulus dialog box as shown below. Then click on "SimGlobalReset" and then on the keyboard click on "R". We can now drive the CLK and the global reset. Pressing the "R" key will toggle the reset.

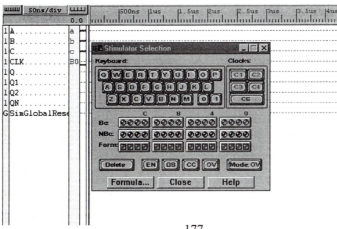

Step 4:
Toggle the "R" and then click on the "footsteps" in the menu bar at the top of the screen. Verify that the outputs follow the truth tables in the text.

Step 5:
You can perform a timing simulation of this same design by simply changing the pull-down menu in the menu bar from "Functional" to "Timing".

Now you can physically verify this design by downloading and testing it as in the "Quick Start OR-Gate lab."

Downloading and Testing Your Design

Step 6:
Download the design to the board as in the "Quick Start OR-Gate lab."

Step 7:
To test the design, use the switches on the board and observe the LEDs. Refer to your lab book to verify which pins are connected to the switches and LEDs.

Step 8:
Look at the mapping report generated by the Implementation tool. Explain how the two shift registers are separated in the device, and whether they have any shared resources.

_____

_____

_____

_____

_____

Step 9: Give a brief explanation of how the circuit works.

_____

_____

_____

_____

_____

Experiment 34
Serial-In, Parallel-Out (SIPO) Shift Register

Introduction

The purpose of this lab is to build, simulate, and download a SIPO register circuit using the Xilinx Foundation tools and Digilab Spartan board.

Objectives

After completing this lab, students will be able to:
- Demonstrate the operation of the circuit described.
- Perform a simple functional and timing simulation using the integrated simulation tool.

Preliminary Procedure

Follow the same steps as in the "Quick Start OR-Gate lab" to set up the lab board.

Procedure

Create a new design with the Xilinx Foundation Series Schematic and name the design SIPO. Consult the pin table for the specific board you are using to determine where to lock the input and output pins. You want to create a design that looks like this:

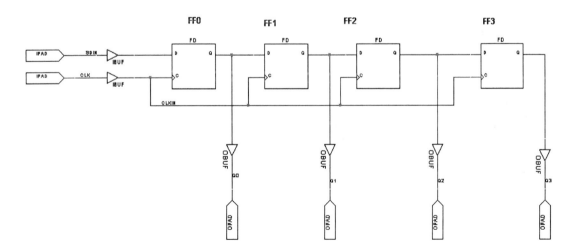

Serial-In, Parallel-Out Shift Register (SIPO)

1) Once you finish creating the desired schematic, make sure to save it. Click **File → Save**. Then return to the Foundation Project Manager (press **<Alt>** + **<Tab>** to task switch).

2) The design entry is finished.

3) Next you need to implement the design the same way as in the Quick Start OR-Gate lab.

4) Click on the Implementation icon in the Project Manager window and follow the same procedure as in previous labs.

HDL Alternative

Here is the code for the lab in VDHL. Follow the design flow in the "Using Hardware Design Languages (HDLs) with Xilinx tools" tutorial. Don't forget to lock the pins in the ".ucf" file.

```
library IEEE;
use IEEE.std_logic_1164.all;

entity sipo is
  port (
    SDIN: in STD_LOGIC;
    CLK: in STD_LOGIC;
    Q: inout STD_LOGIC_VECTOR (3 downto 0)  -- Q defined as an inout
  );                            -- since Q is used as both
end sipo;                              -- and input and output

architecture rtl of sipo is
begin
  shift_register: process(CLK)
  begin
    if (CLK'event and CLK='1') then
      Q <= Q(2 downto 0) & SDIN;   -- Q assigned to the lower 3
    end if;                -- bits concatenated with DIN (&)
  end process shift_register;
end rtl;
```

Here is the code for the same design, this time in the Verilog HDL:

```verilog
module siso (DINR, DINL, CLK, DOUTR, DOUTL);
    input DINR;
    input DINL;
    input CLK;
    output DOUTR;
    output DOUTL;

    reg DOUTR;
    reg DOUTL;
    reg [3:0] rreg;
    reg [3:0] lreg;

    always @(posedge CLK)
        begin: right_shift_register
            DOUTR = rreg[3];
            rreg = {rreg[2:0], DINR};
        end

    always @(posedge CLK)
        begin: left_shift_register
            DOUTL = lreg[0];
            lreg = {DINL, lreg[3:1]};
        end
endmodule
```

Briefly describe the similarities and differences between the VHDL and Verilog versions of the design:

_____

_____

_____

_____

Activity Sheet Experiment 34
Serial-In, Parallel-Out (SIPO) Shift Register Lab

Name: _____

Date: _____

Using the Simulator

Step 1:
To simulate the operation of the circuits, first click on the SIM icon in the menu bar at the top of the schematic screen. The Logic Simulator will open.

Step 2:
Next, click on Signal -> Add Signals in the menu bar at the top of the simulator screen. Here you can decide which signals to drive and observe during the simulation. Note that the signals available are SDin and CLK, as well as the outputs: Q0 through Q3 (from the schematic), and SimGlobalReset. Recall that what SimGlobalReset does is to simulate a global reset on the PLD. It is always a good idea to use this initially just to ensure that you have a totally reset simulation before you start to drive signals.
Double-click on all of the signals (there will be a red checkmark to indicate selection). Then click on CLOSE at the bottom of the screen.

Step 3:
Now click on Signals -> Add Stimulators in the menu bar at the top of the simulator screen. A box that looks like a keyboard will open. Click on the signal "SDin" in the upper-left portion of the screen and then on the "A" on the keyboard (on the screen).
To stimulate the clock, select the CLK signal from the list and then click on the "B$_C$: 0" button below the "0" in the stimulus dialog box as shown below. Then click on "SimGlobalReset" and then on the keyboard click on "R". We can now drive the CLK and the global reset. Pressing the "R" key will toggle the reset.

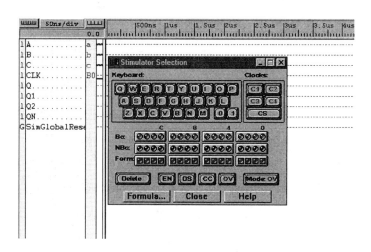

Step 4:
Toggle the "R" and then click on the "footsteps" in the menu bar at the top of the screen. Verify that the outputs follow the truth tables in the text.

Step 5:
You can perform a timing simulation of this same design by simply changing the pull-down menu in the menu bar from "Functional" to "Timing".

Now you can physically verify this design by downloading and testing it as in the "Quick Start OR-Gate lab."

Downloading and Testing Your Design

Step 6:
Download the design to the board as in the "Quick Start OR-Gate lab."

Step 7:
To test the design, use the switches on the board and observe the LEDs. Refer to your lab book to verify which pins are connected to the switches and LEDs.

Step 8:
Give a brief explanation of how the circuit works.

_____

_____

_____

_____

_____

Experiment 35
Serial-to-Parallel Data Converter Lab

Introduction

The purpose of this lab is to build, simulate, and download a serial-to-parallel data conversion circuit using the Xilinx Foundation tools and Digilab Spartan board.

Objectives

After completing this lab, students will be able to:
- Demonstrate the operation of the circuit described.
- Perform a simple functional and timing simulation using the integrated simulation tool.

Preliminary Procedure

Follow the same steps as in the "Quick Start OR-Gate lab" to set up the lab board.

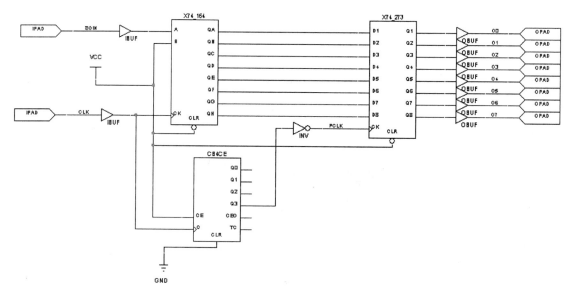

Serial-to-Parallel Data Converter

Figure 1

Procedure

Create a new design with the Xilinx Foundation Series Schematic and name the design SPDC. Consult the pin table for the specific board you are using to determine where to lock the input and output pins.
You want to create a design that looks like Figure 1 on the previous page.

1) To connect the inputs and the outputs to the symbols and wires, this schematic uses a "bus." This is simply a way of drawing several wires as one and saves a lot of time if you need more than 4 wires into a symbol that are all related such as address or data lines. To draw or connect a bus, use the Bus icon.

2) Then you have to name the bus such that it has enough names (such as I0, I1, I2, etc.) to satisfy the number of wires that are being represented. You can do this by double clicking on the bus itself and a window will open that already has the bus range (number of wires) on it and you will have to name it. In this case the output bus (after the OBUF) was named O[7:0]. This is an 8-bit bus consisting of the data input signals. You also need to name each separate wire that connects to the bus so that the software knows how to route and simulate the design.

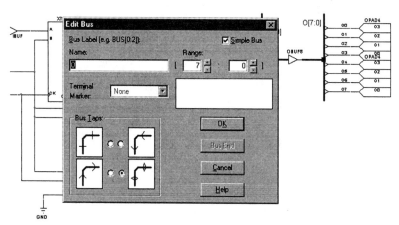

Serial-to-Parallel Data Converter

3) Once you finish creating the desired schematic, make sure to save it. <u>Click</u> **File → Save**. Then return to the Foundation Project Manager (press **<Alt>** + **<Tab>** to task switch).

4) The design entry is finished.

5) Next you need to implement the design the same way as in the Quick Start OR-Gate lab.

6) Click on the Implementation icon in the Project Manager window and follow the same procedure as in previous labs.

Activity Sheet Experiment 35
Serial-to-Parallel Data Converter Lab

Name: _____

Date: _____

Using the Simulator

Step 1:
To simulate the operation of the circuits, first click on the SIM icon in the menu bar at the top of the schematic screen. The Logic Simulator will open.

Step 2:
Next, click on Signal -> Add Signals in the menu bar at the top of the simulator screen. Here you can decide which signals to drive and observe during the simulation. Note that the signals available are SDIN and CLK, as well as the outputs O[7:0] (from the schematic) and SimGlobalReset. Recall that what SimGlobalReset does is to simulate a global reset on the PLD. It is always a good idea to use this initially just to ensure that you have a totally reset simulation before you start to drive signals.
Double-click on all of the signals (there will be a red checkmark to indicate selection).
To "flatten" the bus signal so that you can drive each wire separately, select the bus name, right-click on the signal, and then select Bus>Flatten. Then click on CLOSE at the bottom of the screen.

Step 3:
Now click on Signals -> Add Stimulators in the menu bar at the top of the simulator screen. A box that looks like a keyboard will open. Select "SDIN" and then click on the "S" on the keyboard screen.
To stimulate the clock, select the CLK signal from the list and then click on the "B_C: 0" button below the "0" in the stimulus dialog box as shown below. Then click on "SimGlobalReset" and then on the keyboard click on "R". We can now drive the SDIN, the CLK, and the global reset. Pressing the "R" key will toggle the reset.

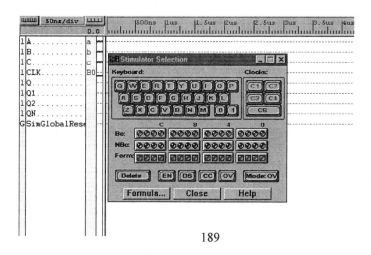

Step 4:

Toggle the "R" and the "SDIN". Next click on the "footsteps" icon in the menu bar at the top of the screen. Verify that the outputs follow the truth table in the text.

Step 5:

You can perform a timing simulation of this same design by simply changing the pull-down menu in the menu bar from "Functional" to "Timing".

Now you can physically verify this design by downloading and testing it as in the "Quickstart OR-Gate lab."

Downloading and Testing Your Design

Step 6:

Download the design to the board as in the "Quickstart OR-Gate lab."

Step 7:

To test the design use the switches on the board and observe the LEDs. Refer to your lab book to verify which pins are connected to the switches and LEDs.

Step 8:

Briefly explain the function of the CB4CE component in this circuit.

_____

_____

_____

_____

_____

Step 9:

Give a brief explanation of how the circuit works.

_____

_____

_____

_____

_____

Experiment 36
Parallel-In, Serial-Out (PISO) Shift Register Lab

Introduction

The purpose of this lab is to build, simulate and download a PISO register circuit using the Xilinx Foundation tools and Digilab Spartan board. This demonstrates how different functions – related or unrelated – can be designed into a single CPLD.

Objectives

After completing this lab, students will be able to:
- Demonstrate the operation of the circuit described.
- Perform a simple functional and timing simulation using the integrated simulation tool.

Preliminary Procedure

Follow the same steps as in the "Quick Start OR-Gate lab" to set up the lab board.

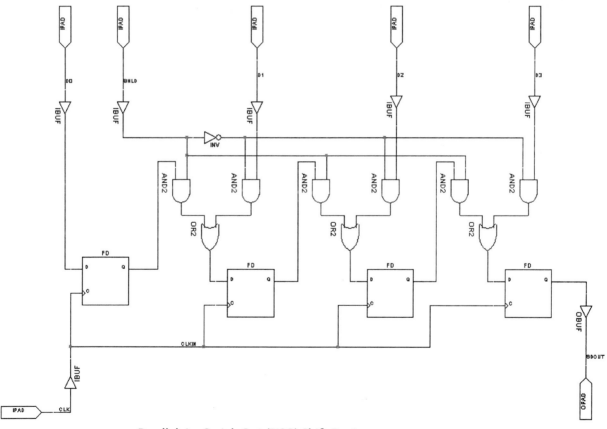

Parallel-In, Serial-Out (PISO) Shift Register

Procedure

Create a new design with the Xilinx Foundation Series Schematic and name the design PISO. Consult the pin table for the specific board you are using to determine where to lock the input and output pins.
You want to create a design that looks like the schematic on the previous page.

1) Once you finish creating the desired schematic, make sure to save it. <u>Click</u> **File → Save**. Then return to the Foundation Project Manager (press **<Alt>** + **<Tab>** to task switch).

2) The design entry is finished.

3) Next you need to implement the design the same way as in the Quick Start OR-Gate lab.

4) Click on the Implementation icon in the Project Manager window and follow the same procedure as in previous labs.

Activity Sheet Experiment 36
Parallel-In, Serial-Out (PISO) Shift Register Lab

Name: _____

Date: _____

Using the Simulator

Step 1:
To simulate the operation of the circuits, first click on the SIM icon in the menu bar at the top of the schematic screen. The Logic Simulator will open.

Step 2:
Next, click on Signal -> Add Signals in the menu bar at the top of the simulator screen. Here you can decide which signals to drive and observe during the simulation. Note that the signals available are SHLD, DO-D3, and CLK, as well as the output SDOUT (from the schematic), and SimGlobalReset. Recall that what SimGlobalReset does is to simulate a global reset on the PLD. It is always a good idea to use this initially just to ensure that you have a totally reset simulation before you start to drive signals.
Double-click on all of the signals (there will be a red checkmark to indicate selection). Then click on CLOSE at the bottom of the screen.

Step 3:
Now click on Signals -> Add Stimulators in the menu bar at the top of the simulator screen. A box that looks like a keyboard will open Click on the signal "D0" in the upper-left portion of the screen and then on the "A" on the keyboard (on the screen). Then click on "D1" in the stimulus list (upper-left corner again) and then on "S" on the keyboard. Continue until you are driving all of the inputs (except CLK).
To stimulate the clock, select the CLK signal from the list and then click on the "B_C: 0" button below the "0" in the stimulus dialog box as shown below. Then click on "SimGlobalReset" and then on the keyboard click on "R". We can now drive the CLK and the global reset. Pressing the "R" key will toggle the reset.

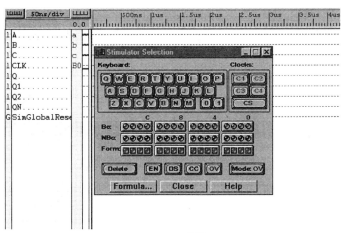

Step 4:
Toggle the "R" and then click on the "footsteps" in the menu bar at the top of the screen. Verify that the outputs follow the truth tables in the text.

Step 5:
You can perform a timing simulation of this same design by simply changing the pull-down menu in the menu bar from "Functional" to "Timing".

Now you can physically verify this design by downloading and testing it as in the "Quick Start OR-Gate lab."

Downloading and Testing Your Design

Step 6:
Download the design to the board as in the "Quick-Start OR-Gate lab."

Step 7:
To test the design, use the switches on the board and observe the LEDs. Refer to your lab book to verify which pins are connected to the switches and LEDs.

Step 8:
Give a brief explanation of how the circuit works.

_____

_____

_____

_____

_____

Experiment 37
Parallel-to-Serial Data Converter Lab

Introduction

The purpose of this lab is to build, simulate and download a parallel-to-serial data conversion circuit using the Xilinx Foundation tools and Digilab Spartan board.

Objectives

After completing this lab, students will be able to:
- Demonstrate the operation of the circuit described.
- Perform a simple functional and timing simulation using the integrated simulation tool.

Preliminary Procedure

Follow the same steps as in the "Quick Start OR-Gate lab" to set up the lab board.

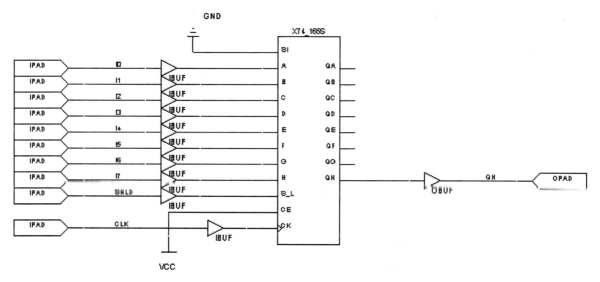

Parallel-to-Serial Data Converter

Figure 1

Procedure

Create a new design with the Xilinx Foundation Series Schematic and name the design PSDC. Consult the pin table for the specific board you are using to determine where to lock the input and output pins.
You want to create a design that looks like the Figure 1 on the previous page.

1) To connect the inputs and the outputs to the symbols and wires this schematic uses a "bus." This is simply a way of drawing several wires as one and saves a lot of time if you need more than 4 wires into a symbol that are all related such as address or data lines. To draw or connect a bus, use the Bus icon.

2) Then you have to name the bus such that it has enough names (such as I0, I1, I2, etc.) to satisfy the number of wires that are being represented. You can do this by double-clicking on the bus itself and a window will open that already has the bus range (number of wires) on it and you will have to name it. In this case the output bus (after the OBUF) was named O[7:0]. This is an 8-bit bus consisting of the data input signals. You also need to name each separate wire that connects to the bus so that the software knows how to route and simulate the design.

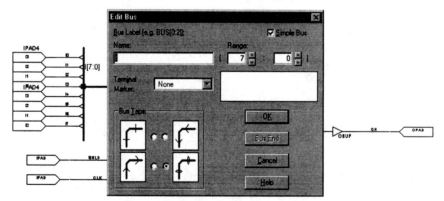

Parallel-to-Serial Data Converter

3) Once you finish creating the desired schematic, make sure to save it. <u>Click</u> **File → Save**. Then return to the Foundation Project Manager (press **<Alt>** + **<Tab>** to task switch).

4) The design entry is finished.

5) Next you need to implement the design the same way as in the Quick Start OR-Gate lab.

6) Click on the Implementation icon in the Project Manager window and follow the same procedure as in previous labs.

Activity Sheet Experiment 37
Parallel-to-Serial Data Converter Lab

Name: _____

Date: _____

Using the Simulator

Step 1:
To simulate the operation of the circuits, first click on the SIM icon in the menu bar at the top of the schematic screen. The Logic Simulator will open.

Step 2:
Next, click on Signal -> Add Signals in the menu bar at the top of the simulator screen. Here you can decide which signals to drive and observe during the simulation. Note that the signals available are I[7:0], SHLD, and CLK, as well as the output QH (from the schematic), and SimGlobalReset. Recall that what SimGlobalReset does is to simulate a global reset on the PLD. It is always a good idea to use this initially just to ensure that you have a totally reset simulation before you start to drive signals.
Double-click on all of the signals (there will be a red checkmark to indicate selection).
To "flatten" the bus signal so that you can drive each wire separately, select the bus name, right-click on the signal, and then select Bus>Flatten. Then click on CLOSE at the bottom of the screen.

Step 3:
Now click on Signals -> Add Stimulators in the menu bar at the top of the simulator screen. A box that looks like a keyboard will open. Select "SHLD" and then click on the "S" on the keyboard screen. Similarly click on "I0" and then select "Q" from the keyboard on the screen. Continue until you have selected all input signals with the exception of CLK.
To stimulate the clock, select the CLK signal from the list and then click on the "B$_C$: 0" button below the "0" in the stimulus dialog box as shown below. Then click on "SimGlobalReset" and then on the keyboard click on "R". We can now drive the SDIN, the CLK, and the global reset. Pressing the "R" key will toggle the reset.

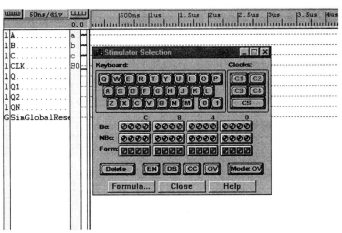

Step 4:
Toggle the "R" and the "SHLD" and the signals on the input bus. Next click on the "footsteps" icon in the menu bar at the top of the screen. Verify that the outputs follow the truth table in the text.

Step 5:
You can perform a timing simulation of this same design by simply changing the pull-down menu in the menu bar from "Functional" to "Timing".

Now you can physically verify this design by testing it as in the "Quick Start OR-Gate lab."

Downloading and Testing Your Design

Step 6:
Download the design to the board as in the "Quick Start OR-Gate lab."

Step 7:
To test the design, use the switches on the board and observe the LEDs. Refer to your lab book to verify which pins are connected to the switches and LEDs.

Step 8:
Give a brief explanation of what the SHLD signal is used for.

_____

_____

_____

_____

_____

Step 9:
Give a brief explanation of how the circuit works.

_____

_____

_____

_____

_____

Experiment 38 Shift-Right Sequence Generator Lab

Introduction

The purpose of this lab is to build, simulate and download a shift-right sequencer circuit using the Xilinx Foundation tools and Digilab Spartan board.

Objectives

After completing this lab, students will be able to:
- Demonstrate the operation of the circuit described.
- Perform a simple functional and timing simulation using the integrated simulation tool

Preliminary Procedure

Follow the same steps as in the "Quick Start OR-Gate lab" to set up the lab board.

Procedure

Create a new design with the Xilinx Foundation Series Schematic and name the design SRSEQ. Consult the pin table for the specific board you are using to determine where to lock the input and output pins.
You want to create a design that looks like Figure 1:

Figure 1

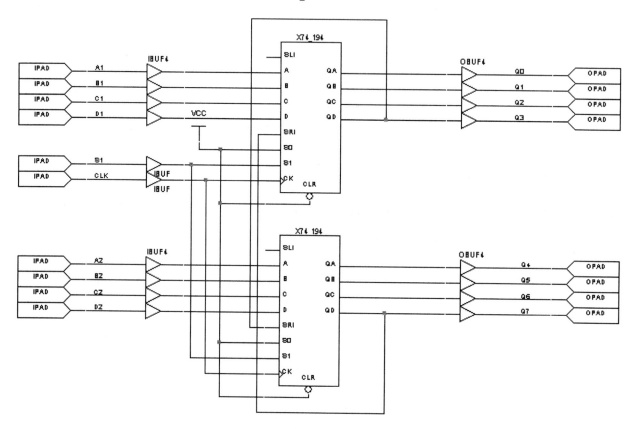

Shift-Right Sequence Generator

1) Once you finish creating the desired schematic, make sure to save it. Click **File → Save**. Then return to the Foundation Project Manager (press <Alt> + <Tab> to task switch).

2) The design entry is finished.

3) Next you need to implement the design the same way as in the Quick Start OR-Gate lab.

4) Click on the Implementation icon in the Project Manager window and follow the same procedure as in previous labs.

Activity Sheet Experiment 38
Shift-Right Sequence Generator Lab

Name: _____

Date: _____

Using the Simulator

Step 1:
To simulate the operation of the circuits, first click on the SIM icon in the menu bar at the top of the schematic screen. The Logic Simulator will open.

Step 2:
Next, click on Signal -> Add Signals in the menu bar at the top of the simulator screen. Here you can decide which signals to drive and observe during the simulation. Note that the signals available are A1,B1,C1,D1,A2,B2,C2,D2, and CLK, as well as the outputs: Q0-Q7 (from the schematic), and SimGlobalReset. Recall that what SimGlobalReset does is to simulate a global reset on the PLD. It is always a good idea to use this initially just to ensure that you have a totally reset simulation before you start to drive signals.
Double-click on all of the signals (there will be a red checkmark to indicate selection). Then click on CLOSE at the bottom of the screen.

Step 3:
Now click on Signals -> Add Stimulators in the menu bar at the top of the simulator screen. A box that looks like a keyboard will open. Click on the signal "A1" in the upper-left portion of the screen and then on the "Q" on the keyboard (on the screen). Do the same for "B1" using the "W" key on the keyboard . Continue in this manner until you are driving all of the inputs except for CLK.
To stimulate the clock, select the CLK signal from the list and then click on the "D0" button below the "0" in the stimulus dialog box as shown below. Then click on "SimGlobalReset" and then on the keyboard click on "R". We can now drive the CLK, the inputs, S1, and the global reset. Pressing the "R" key will toggle the reset.

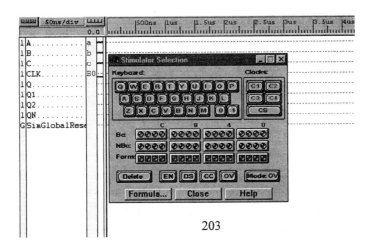

203

Step 4:
Toggle the "R" and then click on the "footsteps" in the menu bar at the top of the screen. Verify that the outputs follow the truth tables in the text.

Step 5:
You can perform a timing simulation of this same design by simply changing the pull-down menu in the menu bar from "Functional" to "Timing".

Now you can physically verify this design by downloading and testing it as in the "Quick Start OR-Gate lab."

Downloading and Testing Your Design

Step 6:
Download the design to the board as in the "Quick Start OR-Gate lab."

Step 7:
To test the design, use the switches on the board and observe the LEDs. Refer to your lab book to verify which pins are connected to the switches and LEDs.

Step 8:
Give a brief explanation of how you could turn the circuit of Figure 1 into a shift-left sequence generator.

_____

_____

_____

_____

_____

Step 9:
Give a brief explanation of how the circuit works.

_____

_____

_____

_____

Experiment 39 Controlled Buffer Register with 3-State Output

Introduction

The purpose of this lab is to build, simulate, and download a controlled buffer register circuit using the Xilinx Foundation tools and Digilab Spartan board. This demonstrates how different functions – related or unrelated – can be designed into a single PLD device.

Objectives

After completing this lab, students will be able to:

- Demonstrate the operation of the circuit described.
- Perform a simple functional and timing simulation using the integrated simulation tool.

Preliminary Procedure

Follow the same steps as in the "Quick Start OR-Gate lab" to set up the lab board.

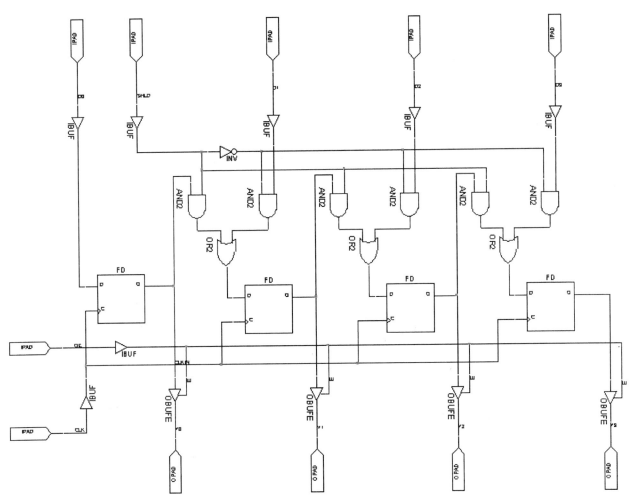

Controlled Buffer Reg. with 3-state Output

Procedure

Create a new design with the Xilinx Foundation Series Schematic and name the design CREG. Consult the pin table for the specific board you are using to determine where to lock the input and output pins. You want to create a design that looks like the schematic on the previous page.

1) Once you finish creating the desired schematic, make sure to save it. <u>Click</u> **File → Save**. Then return to the Foundation Project Manager (press **<Alt>** + **<Tab>** to task switch).

2) The design entry is finished.

3) Next you need to implement the design the same way as in the Quick Start OR-Gate lab.

4) Click on the Implementation icon in the Project Manager window and follow the same procedure as in previous labs.

Activity Sheet Experiment 39
Controlled Buffer Register with 3-State Output

Name: _____

Date: _____

Using the Simulator

Step 1:
To simulate the operation of the circuits, first click on the SIM icon in the menu bar at the top of the schematic screen. The Logic Simulator will open.

Step 2:
Next, click on Signal -> Add Signals in the menu bar at the top of the simulator screen. Here you can decide which signals to drive and observe during the simulation. Note that the signals available are SHLD, DO-D3, OE, and CLK, as well as the outputs Y0-Y3 (from the schematic), and SimGlobalReset. Recall that what SimGlobalReset does is to simulate a global reset on the PLD. It is always a good idea to use this initially just to ensure that you have a totally reset simulation before you start to drive signals.
Double-click on all of the signals (there will be a red checkmark to indicate selection). Then click on CLOSE at the bottom of the screen.

Step 3:
Now click on Signals -> Add Stimulators in the menu bar at the top of the simulator screen. A box that looks like a keyboard will open. Click on the signal "D0" in the upper-left portion of the screen and then on the "A" on the keyboard (on the screen). Then click on "D1" in the stimulus list (upper-left corner again) and then on "S" on the keyboard. Continue until you are driving all of the inputs (except CLK).
To stimulate the clock select the CLK signal from the list and then click on the "B$_C$: 0" button below the "0" in the stimulus dialog box as shown below. Then click on "SimGlobalReset" and then on the keyboard click on "R". We can now drive the CLK and the global reset. Pressing the "R" key will toggle the reset.

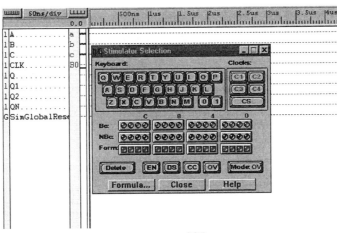

Step 4:
Toggle the "R" and then click on the "footsteps" in the menu bar at the top of the screen. Verify that the outputs follow the truth tables in the text.

Step 5:
You can perform a timing simulation of this same design by simply changing the pull-down menu in the menu bar from "Functional" to "Timing".

Now you can physically verify this design by downloading and testing it as in the "Quick Start OR-Gate lab."

Downloading and Testing Your Design

Step 6:
Download the design to the board as in the "Quick Start OR-Gate lab."

Step 7:
To test the design, use the switches on the board and observe the LEDs. Refer to your lab book to verify which pins are connected to the switches and LEDs.

Step 8:
Give a brief explanation of how the circuit works.

_____

_____

_____

_____

_____

Experiment 40 Ring Counter Lab

Introduction

The purpose of this lab is to build, simulate, and download a ring counter circuit using the Xilinx Foundation tools and Digilab Spartan Board. This demonstrates how different functions – related or unrelated – can be designed into a single PLD.

Objectives

After completing this lab, students will be able to:

- Demonstrate the operation of the circuit described.
- Perform a simple functional and timing simulation using the integrated simulation tool.

Preliminary Procedure

Follow the same steps as in the "Quick Start OR-Gate lab" to set up the lab board.

Figure 1

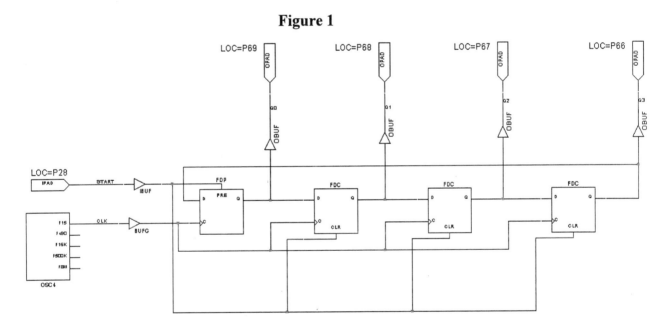

Ring Counter

Procedure

Create a new design with the Xilinx Foundation Series Schematic and name the design RING. You want to create a design that looks like Figure 1 on the previous page. Use the pin mapping sheet for the specific board you are using to select pins for the inputs and outputs of the design.

1) Once you finish creating the desired schematic, make sure to save it. <u>Click</u> **File → Save**. Then return to the Foundation Project Manager (press **<Alt>** + **<Tab>** to task switch).

2) The design entry is finished.

3) Next you need to implement the design the same way as in the Quick Start OR-Gate lab.

4) Click on the Implementation icon in the Project Manager window and follow the same procedure as in previous labs.

Activity Sheet Experiment 40
Ring Counter Lab

Name: _____

Date: _____

Using the Simulator

Step 1:
To simulate the operation of the circuits, first click on the SIM icon in the menu bar at the top of the schematic screen. The Logic Simulator will open.

Step 2:
Next, click on Signal -> Add Signals in the menu bar at the top of the simulator screen. Here you can decide which signals to drive and observe during the simulation. Note that the signals available are START and CLK, as well as the outputs Q0-Q3 (from the schematic), and SimGlobalReset. Recall that what SimGlobalReset does is to simulate a global reset on the PLD. It is always a good idea to use this initially just to ensure that you have a totally reset simulation before you start to drive signals.
Double-click on all of the signals (there will be a red checkmark to indicate selection). Then click on CLOSE at the bottom of the screen.

Step 3:
Now click on Signals -> Add Stimulators in the menu bar at the top of the simulator screen. A box that looks like a keyboard will open. Click on the signal "START" in the upper-left portion of the screen and then on the "A" on the keyboard (on the screen).
To stimulate the clock, select the CLK signal from the list and then click on the "B0" button below the "0" in the stimulus dialog box as shown below. Then click on "SimGlobalReset" and then on the keyboard click on "R". We can now drive the START, the CLK, and the global reset. Pressing the "R" key will toggle the reset.

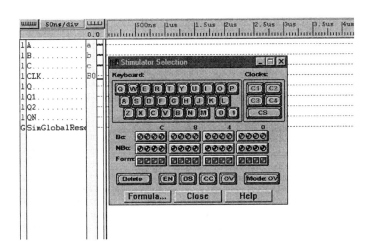

Step 4:
Toggle the "R" and then the "START" click on the "footsteps" in the menu bar at the top of the screen. Verify that the outputs follow the truth tables in the text.

Step 5:
You can perform a timing simulation of this same design by simply changing the pull-down menu in the menu bar from "Functional" to "Timing". Now you can physically verify this design by downloading and testing it as in the "Quick Start OR-Gate lab."

Downloading and Testing Your Design

Step 6:
Download the design to the board as in the "Quick Start OR-Gate lab."

Step 7:
To test the design, use the switches on the board and observe the LEDs. Refer to your lab book to verify which pins are connected to the switches and LEDs.

Step 8:
Give a brief explanation of how the circuit works.

_____

_____

_____

_____

_____

Experiment 41 8-Bit Ring Counter Lab

Introduction

The purpose of this lab is to build, simulate, and download an 8-bit ring counter circuit using the Xilinx Foundation tools and Digilab Spartan Board. This demonstrates how different functions – related or unrelated – can be designed into a single PLD.

Objectives

After completing this lab, students will be able to:

- Demonstrate the operation of the circuit described.
- Perform a simple functional and timing simulation using the integrated simulation tool.

Preliminary Procedure

Follow the same steps as in the "Quick Start OR-Gate lab" to set up the lab board.

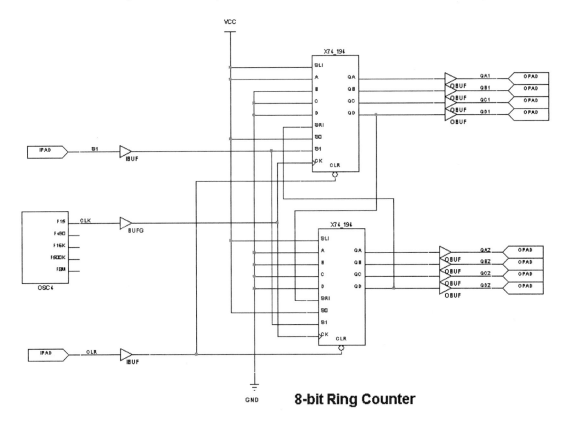

8-bit Ring Counter

Figure 1

Procedure

Create a new design with the Xilinx Foundation Series Schematic and name the design RING8. You want to create a design that looks like Figure 1 on the previous page. Use the pin mapping sheet for the specific board you are using to select pins for the inputs and outputs of the design.

1) Once you finish creating the desired schematic, make sure to save it. <u>Click</u> **File → Save**. Then return to the Foundation Project Manager (press **<Alt>** + **<Tab>** to task switch).

2) The design entry is finished.

3) Next you need to implement the design the same way as in the Quick Start OR-Gate lab.

4) Click on the Implementation icon in the Project Manager window and follow the same procedure as in previous labs.

Activity Sheet Experiment 41
8-Bit Ring Counter Lab

Name: _____

Date: _____

Using the Simulator

Step 1:
To simulate the operation of the circuits, first click on the SIM icon in the menu bar at the top of the schematic screen. The Logic Simulator will open.

Step 2:
Next, click on Signal -> Add Signals in the menu bar at the top of the simulator screen. Here you can decide which signals to drive and observe during the simulation. Note that the signals available are S1, CLR, and CLK, as well as the outputs QA1-QD1 and QA2-QD2 (from the schematic), and SimGlobalReset. Recall that what SimGlobalReset does is to simulate a global reset on the PLD. It is always a good idea to use this initially just to ensure that you have a totally reset simulation before you start to drive signals.
Double-click on all of the signals (there will be a red checkmark to indicate selection). Then click on CLOSE at the bottom of the screen.

Step 3:
Now click on Signals -> Add Stimulators in the menu bar at the top of the simulator screen. A box that looks like a keyboard will open. Click on the signal "S1" in the upper-left portion of the screen and then on the "A" on the keyboard (on the screen). Then click on "CLR" in the stimulus window and click on "S" in the keyboard window.
To stimulate the clock, select the CLK signal from the list and then click on the "B$_C$: 0" button below the "0" in the stimulus dialog box as shown below. Then click on "SimGlobalReset" and then on the keyboard click on "R". We can now drive the START, the CLK, and the global reset. Pressing the "R" key will toggle the reset.

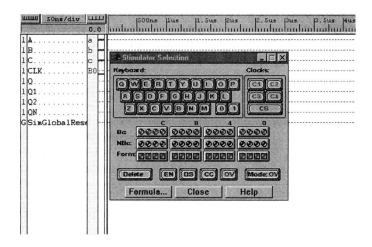

Step 4:
Toggle the "R" and then the "S1" and "CLR". Next click on the "footsteps" icon in the menu bar at the top of the screen. Verify that the outputs follow the truth tables in the text.

Step 5:
You can perform a timing simulation of this same design by simply changing the pull-down menu in the menu bar from "Functional" to "Timing". Now you can physically verify this design by downloading and testing it as in the "Quick Start OR-Gate lab."

Downloading and Testing Your Design

Step 6:
Download the design to the XS95 board as in the "Quick Start OR-Gate lab."

Step 7:
To test the design use the switches on the board and observe the LEDs. Refer to your lab book to verify which pins are connected to the switches and LEDs.

Step 8:
Give a brief explanation of how the circuit works.

_____

_____

_____

_____

_____

Experiment 42 Johnson Counter Lab

Introduction

The purpose of this lab is to build, simulate, and download a Johnson counter circuit using the Xilinx Foundation tools and Digilab Spartan board. This lab demonstrates how different functions – related or unrelated – can be designed into a single PLD.

Objectives

After completing this lab, students will be able to:
- Demonstrate the operation of the circuit described.
- Perform a simple functional and timing simulation using the integrated simulation tool.

Preliminary Procedure

Follow the same steps as in the "Quick Start OR-Gate lab" to set up the lab board.

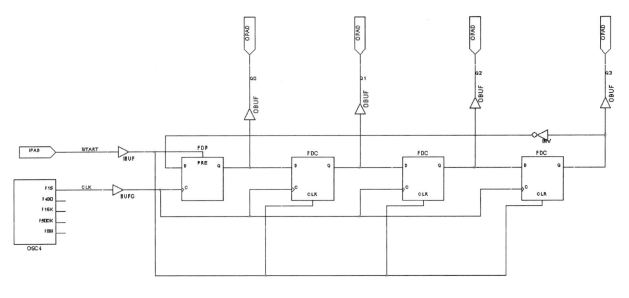

Johnson Counter

Figure 1

Procedure

Create a new design with the Xilinx Foundation Series Schematic and name the design JOHN4. You want to create a design that looks like Figure 1

above. Use the pin mapping sheet for the specific board you are using to select pins for the inputs and outputs of the design.

1) Once you finish creating the desired schematic, make sure to save it. Click **File → Save**. Then return to the Foundation Project Manager (press **<Alt>** + **<Tab>** to task switch).

2) The design entry is finished.

3) Next you need to implement the design the same way as in the Quick Start OR-Gate lab.

4) Click on the Implementation icon in the Project Manager window and follow the same procedure as in previous labs.

Activity Sheet Experiment 42
Johnson Counter Lab

Name: _____

Date: _____

Using the Simulator

Step 1:
To simulate the operation of the circuits, first click on the SIM icon in the menu bar at the top of the schematic screen. The Logic Simulator will open.

Step 2:
Next, click on Signal -> Add Signals in the menu bar at the top of the simulator screen. Here you can decide which signals to drive and observe during the simulation. Note that the signals available are START and CLK, as well as the outputs Q0-Q3 (from the schematic), and SimGlobalReset. Recall that what SimGlobalReset does is to simulate a global reset on the PLD. It is always a good idea to use this initially just to ensure that you have a totally reset simulation before you start to drive signals.
Double-click on all of the signals (there will be a red checkmark to indicate selection). Then click on CLOSE at the bottom of the screen.

Step 3:
Now click on Signals -> Add Stimulators in the menu bar at the top of the simulator screen. A box that looks like a keyboard will open. Click on the signal "START" in the upper-left portion of the screen and then on the "A" on the keyboard (on the screen).
To stimulate the clock, select the CLK signal from the list and then click on the "B_C: 0" button below the "0" in the stimulus dialog box as shown below. Then click on "SimGlobalReset" and then on the keyboard click on "R". We can now drive the START, the CLK, and the global reset. Pressing the "R" key will toggle the reset.

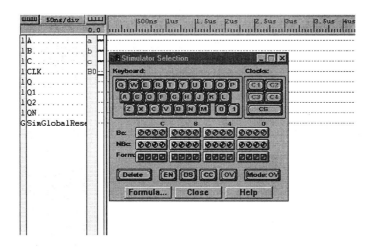

Step 4:
Toggle the "R" and then the "S1" and "CLR". Next click on the "footsteps" icon in the menu bar at the top of the screen. Verify that the outputs follow the truth tables in the text.

Step 5:
You can perform a timing simulation of this same design by simply changing the pull-down menu in the menu bar from "Functional" to "Timing". Now you can physically verify this design by downloading and testing it as in the "Quick Start OR-Gate lab."

Downloading and Testing Your Design

Step 6:
Download the design to the board as in the "Quick Start OR-Gate lab."

Step 7:
To test the design, use the switches on the board and observe the LEDs. Refer to your lab book to verify which pins are connected to the switches and LEDs.

Step 8:
Give a brief explanation of how the Johnson counter differs from the ring counter of the previous two labs.

_____

_____

_____

_____

Step 9:
Give a brief explanation of how the circuit works.

_____

_____

_____

_____

Experiment 43
Asynchronous Binary Up-Counter Lab

Introduction

The purpose of this lab is to build, simulate, and download a counter circuit using the Xilinx Foundation tools and Digilab Spartan Board.

Objectives

After completing this lab, students will be able to:
- Demonstrate the operation of the circuit described.
- Perform a simple functional and timing simulation using the integrated simulation tool.

Preliminary Procedure

Follow the same steps as in the "Quick Start OR-Gate lab" to set up the lab board.

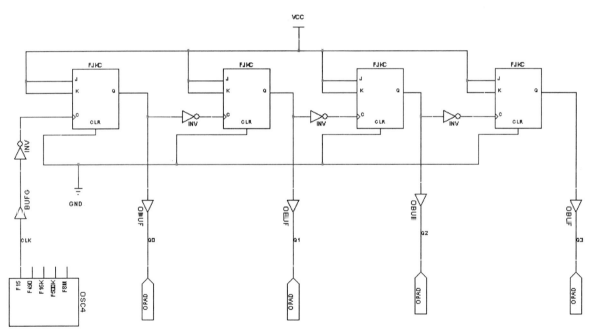

Asynchronous Binary Up Counter

Figure 1

Procedure

Create a new design with the Xilinx Foundation Series Schematic and name the design ABUP. You want to create a design that looks like Figure 1. Use the pin mapping sheet for the specific board you are using to select pins for the inputs and outputs of the design.

1) Once you finish creating the desired schematic, make sure to save it. Click **File → Save**. Then return to the Foundation Project Manager (press **<Alt>** + **<Tab>** to task switch).

2) The design entry is finished.

3) Next you need to implement the design the same way as in the Quick Start OR-Gate lab.

4) Click on the Implementation icon in the Project Manager window and follow the same procedure as in previous labs.

Activity Sheet Experiment 43
Asynchronous Binary Up-Counter Lab

Name: _____

Date: _____

Using the Simulator

Step 1:
To simulate the operation of the circuits, first click on the SIM icon in the menu bar at the top of the schematic screen. The Logic Simulator will open.

Step 2:
Next, click on Signal -> Add Signals in the menu bar at the top of the simulator screen. Here you can decide which signals to drive and observe during the simulation. Note that the signals available are CLK, as well as the outputs Q0-Q3 (from the schematic), and SimGlobalReset. Recall that what SimGlobalReset does is to simulate a global reset on the PLD. It is always a good idea to use this initially just to ensure that you have a totally reset simulation before you start to drive signals.
Double-click on all of the signals (there will be a red checkmark to indicate selection). Then click on CLOSE at the bottom of the screen.

Step 3:
Now click on Signals -> Add Stimulators in the menu bar at the top of the simulator screen. A box that looks like a keyboard will open.
To stimulate the clock, select the CLK signal from the list and then click on the "B_C: 0" button below the "0" in the stimulus dialog box as shown below. Then click on "SimGlobalReset" and then on the keyboard click on "R". We can now drive the CTRL, the CLK, and the global reset. Pressing the "R" key will toggle the reset.

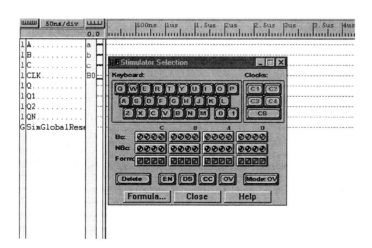

223

Step 4:
Toggle the "R" and the "CTRL". Next click on the "footsteps" icon in the menu bar at the top of the screen. Verify that the outputs follow the truth tables in the text.

Step 5:
You can perform a timing simulation of this same design by simply changing the pull-down menu in the menu bar from "Functional" to "Timing". Now you can physically verify this design by downloading and testing it as in the "Quick Start OR-Gate lab."

Downloading and Testing Your Design

Step 6:
Download the design to the board as in the "Quick Start OR-Gate lab."

Step 7:
To test the design, use the switches on the board and observe the LEDs. Refer to your lab book to verify which pins are connected to the switches and LEDs.

Step 8:
Give a brief explanation of the term *asynchronous*.

_____

_____

_____

_____

Step 9:
Give a brief explanation of how the circuit works.

_____

_____

_____

_____

Experiment 44 Asynchronous Binary Down-Counter Lab

Introduction

The purpose of this lab is to build, simulate, and download a counter circuit using the Xilinx Foundation tools and Digilab Spartan board.

Objectives

After completing this lab, students will be able to:
- Demonstrate the operation of the circuit described.
- Perform a simple functional and timing simulation using the integrated simulation tool.

Preliminary Procedure

Follow the same steps as in the "Quick Start OR-Gate lab" to set up the lab board.

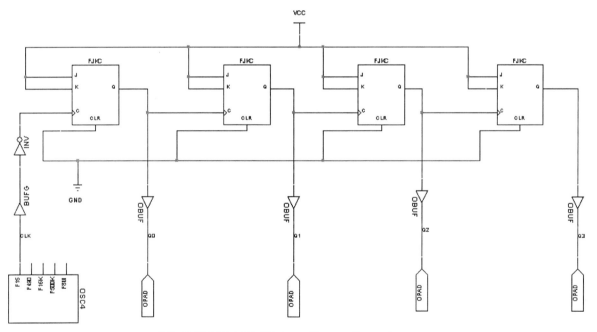

Asynchronous Binary Down Counter

Figure 1

Procedure

Create a new design with the Xilinx Foundation Series Schematic and name the design ABDN. You want to create a design that looks like Figure 1. Use the pin mapping sheet for the specific board you are using to select pins for the inputs and outputs of the design.

1) Once you finish creating the desired schematic, make sure to save it. Click **File → Save**. Then return to the Foundation Project Manager (press **<Alt>** + **<Tab>** to task switch).

2) The design entry is finished.

3) Next you need to implement the design the same way as in the Quick Start OR-Gate lab.

4) Click on the Implementation icon in the Project Manager window and follow the same procedure as in previous labs.

Activity Sheet Experiment 44
Asynchronous Binary Down-Counter Lab

Name: _____

Date: _____

Using the Simulator

Step 1:
To simulate the operation of the circuits, first click on the SIM icon in the menu bar at the top of the schematic screen. The Logic Simulator will open.

Step 2:
Next, click on Signal -> Add Signals in the menu bar at the top of the simulator screen. Here you can decide which signals to drive and observe during the simulation. Note that the signals available are CLK, as well as the outputs Q0-Q3 (from the schematic), and SimGlobalReset. Recall that what SimGlobalReset does is to simulate a global reset on the PLD. It is always a good idea to use this initially just to ensure that you have a totally reset simulation before you start to drive signals.
Double-click on all of the signals (there will be a red checkmark to indicate selection). Then click on CLOSE at the bottom of the screen.

Step 3:
Now click on Signals -> Add Stimulators in the menu bar at the top of the simulator screen. A box that looks like a keyboard will open.
To stimulate the clock, select the CLK signal from the list and then click on the "B$_C$: 0" button below the "0" in the stimulus dialog box as shown below. Then click on "SimGlobalReset" and then on the keyboard click on "R". We can now drive the CTRL, the CLK, and the global reset. Pressing the "R" key will toggle the reset.

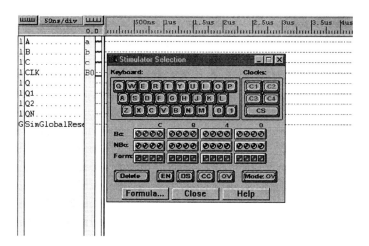

Step 4:

Toggle the "R" and the "CTRL". Next click on the "footsteps" icon in the menu bar at the top of the screen. Verify that the outputs follow the truth tables in the text.

Step 5:

You can perform a timing simulation of this same design by simply changing the pull-down menu in the menu bar from "Functional" to "Timing". Now you can physically verify this design by downloading and testing it as in the "Quick Start OR-Gate lab."

Downloading and Testing Your Design

Step 6:

Download the design to the board as in the "Quick Start OR-Gate lab."

Step 7:

To test the design, use the switches on the board and observe the LEDs. Refer to your lab book to verify which pins are connected to the switches and LEDs.

Step 8:

Give a brief explanation of how the circuit works.

_____

_____

_____

_____

Experiment 45 Asynchronous Binary Up/Down Counter Lab

Introduction

The purpose of this lab is to build, simulate, and download a counter circuit using the Xilinx Foundation tools and Digilab Spartan board.

Objectives

After completing this lab, students will be able to:
- Demonstrate the operation of the circuit described.
- Perform a simple functional and timing simulation using the integrated simulation tool.

Preliminary Procedure

Follow the same steps as in the "Quick Start OR-Gate lab" to set up the lab board.

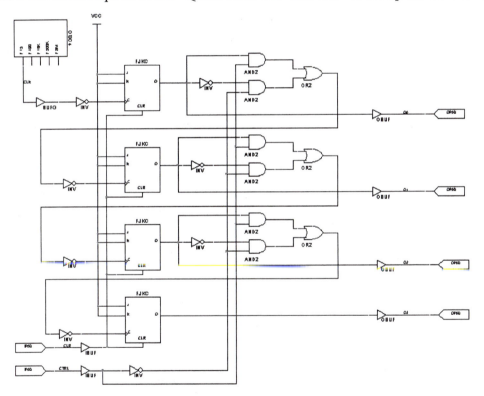

Asynchronous Binary Up/Down Counter

Figure 1

Procedure

Create a new design with the Xilinx Foundation Series Schematic and name the design ABUD. You want to create a design that looks like Figure 1. Use the pin mapping sheet for the specific board you are using to select pins for the inputs and outputs of the design.

1) Once you finish creating the desired schematic, make sure to save it. Click **File → Save**. Then return to the Foundation Project Manager (press **<Alt>** + **<Tab>** to task switch).

2) The design entry is finished.

3) Next you need to implement the design the same way as in the Quick Start OR-Gate lab.

4) Click on the Implementation icon in the Project Manager window and follow the same procedure as in previous labs.

Activity Sheet Experiment 45
Asynchronous Binary Up/Down Counter Lab

Name: _____

Date: _____

Using the Simulator

Step 1:
To simulate the operation of the circuits, first click on the SIM icon in the menu bar at the top of the schematic screen. The Logic Simulator will open.

Step 2:
Next, click on Signal -> Add Signals in the menu bar at the top of the simulator screen. Here you can decide which signals to drive and observe during the simulation. Note that the signals available are CTRL and CLK, as well as the outputs Q0-Q3 (from the schematic), and SimGlobalReset. Recall that what SimGlobalReset does is to simulate a global reset on the PLD. It is always a good idea to use this initially just to ensure that you have a totally reset simulation before you start to drive signals.
Double-click on all of the signals (there will be a red checkmark to indicate selection). Then click on CLOSE at the bottom of the screen.

Step 3:
Now click on Signals -> Add Stimulators in the menu bar at the top of the simulator screen. A box that looks like a keyboard will open. Click on "CTRL" in the stimulus window and then on "A" on the keyboard screen.
To stimulate the clock, select the CLK signal from the list and then click on the "B_C: 0" button below the "0" in the stimulus dialog box as shown below. Then click on "SimGlobalReset" and then on the keyboard click on "R". We can now drive the CTRL, the CLK, and the global reset. Pressing the "R" key will toggle the reset

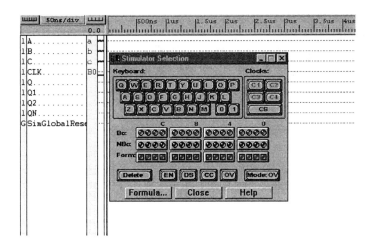

231

Step 4:

Toggle the "R" and the "CTRL". Next click on the "footsteps" icon in the menu bar at the top of the screen. Verify that the outputs follow the truth tables in the text.

Step 5:

You can perform a timing simulation of this same design by simply changing the pull-down menu in the menu bar from "Functional" to "Timing". Now you can physically verify this design by downloading and testing it as in the "Quick Start OR-Gate lab."

Downloading and Testing Your Design

Step 6:

Download the design to the board as in the "Quick Start OR-Gate lab."

Step 7:

To test the design, use the switches on the board and observe the LEDs. Refer to your lab book to verify which pins are connected to the switches and LEDs.

Step 8:

Give a brief explanation of how the circuit works.

_____

_____

_____

_____

Experiment 46 Asynchronous Decade Counter Lab

Introduction

The purpose of this lab is to build, simulate, and download a counter circuit using the Xilinx Foundation tools and Digilab Spartan board.

Objectives

After completing this lab, students will be able to:

- Demonstrate the operation of the circuit described.
- Perform a simple functional and timing simulation using the integrated simulation tool.

Preliminary Procedure

Follow the same steps as in the "Quick Start OR-Gate lab" to set up the lab board.

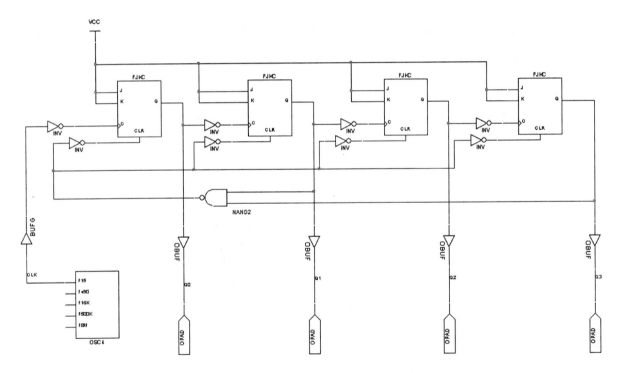

Asynchronous Decade Counter

Figure 1

Procedure

Create a new design with the Xilinx Foundation Series Schematic and name the design DEC. You want to create a design that looks like Figure 1. Use the pin mapping sheet for the specific board you are using to select pins for the inputs and outputs of the design.

1) Once you finish creating the desired schematic, make sure to save it. <u>Click</u> **File → Save**. Then return to the Foundation Project Manager (press **<Alt>** + **<Tab>** to task switch).

2) The design entry is finished.

3) Next, you need to implement the design the same way as in the Quick Start OR-Gate lab.

4) Click on the Implementation icon in the Project Manager window and follow the same procedure as in previous labs.

Activity Sheet Experiment 46
Asynchronous Decade Counter Lab

Name: _____

Date: _____

Using the Simulator

Step 1:
To simulate the operation of the circuits, first click on the SIM icon in the menu bar at the top of the schematic screen. The Logic Simulator will open.

Step 2:
Next, click on Signal -> Add Signals in the menu bar at the top of the simulator screen. Here you can decide which signals to drive and observe during the simulation. Note that the signals available are CLK, as well as the outputs Q0-Q3 (from the schematic), and SimGlobalReset. Recall that what SimGlobalReset does is to simulate a global reset on the PLD. It is always a good idea to use this initially just to ensure that you have a totally reset simulation before you start to drive signals.
Double-click on all of the signals (there will be a red checkmark to indicate selection). Then click on CLOSE at the bottom of the screen.

Step 3:
Now click on Signals -> Add Stimulators in the menu bar at the top of the simulator screen. A box that looks like a keyboard will open.
To stimulate the clock select the CLK signal from the list and then click on the "B_C: 0" button below the "0" in the stimulus dialog box as shown below. Then click on "SimGlobalReset" and then on the keyboard click on "R". We can now drive the CTRL, the CLK, and the global reset. Pressing the "R" key will toggle the reset.

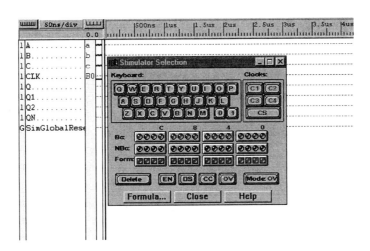

235

Step 4:

Toggle the "R" and the "CTRL". Next click on the "footsteps" icon in the menu bar at the top of the screen. Verify that the outputs follow the truth tables in the text.

Step 5:

You can perform a timing simulation of this same design by simply changing the pull-down menu in the menu bar from "Functional" to "Timing". Note that the clock doesn't count correctly unless you use the timing simulation. Why is this?

Now you can physically verify this design by downloading and testing it as in the "Quick Start OR-Gate lab."

Downloading and Testing Your Design

Step 6:

Download the design to the board as in the "Quick Start OR-Gate lab."

Step 7:

To test the design, use the switches on the board and observe the LEDs. Refer to your lab book to verify which pins are connected to the switches and LEDs.

Step 8:

Give a brief explanation of how the circuit works.

_____

_____

_____

_____

Experiment 47 Asynchronous Presettable Counter Lab

Introduction

The purpose of this lab is to build, simulate, and download a counter circuit using the Xilinx Foundation tools and Digilab Spartan board.

Objectives

After completing this lab, students will be able to:
- Demonstrate the operation of the circuit described.
- Perform a simple functional and timing simulation using the integrated simulation tool.

Preliminary Procedure

Follow the same steps as in the "Quick Start OR-Gate lab" to set up the lab board.

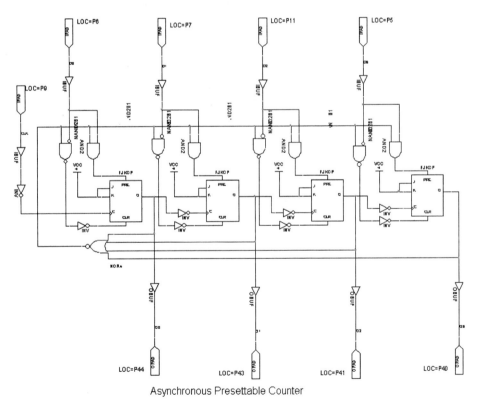

Asynchronous Presettable Counter

Figure 1

Procedure

Create a new design with the Xilinx Foundation Series Schematic and name the design PRE. You want to create a design that looks like Figure 1. Use the pin mapping sheet for the specific board you are using to select pins for the inputs and outputs of the design.

1) Once you finish creating the desired schematic, make sure to save it. <u>Click</u> **File → Save**. Then return to the Foundation Project Manager (press **<Alt>** + **<Tab>** to task switch).

2) The design entry is finished.

3) Next you need to implement the design the same way as in the Quick Start OR-Gate lab.

4) Click on the Implementation icon in the Project Manager window and follow the same procedure as in previous labs.

Activity Sheet Experiment 47
Asynchronous Presettable Counter Lab

Name: _____

Date: _____

Using the Simulator

Step 1:
To simulate the operation of the circuits, first click on the SIM icon in the menu bar at the top of the schematic screen. The Logic Simulator will open.

Step 2:
Next, click on Signal -> Add Signals in the menu bar at the top of the simulator screen. Here you can decide which signals to drive and observe during the simulation. Note that the signals available are D0-D3 and CLK, as well as the outputs Q0-Q3 (from the schematic), and SimGlobalReset. Recall that what SimGlobalReset does is to simulate a global reset on the PLD. It is always a good idea to use this initially just to ensure that you have a totally reset simulation before you start to drive signals.
Double-click on all of the signals (there will be a red checkmark to indicate selection). Then click on CLOSE at the bottom of the screen.

Step 3:
Now click on Signals -> Add Stimulators in the menu bar at the top of the simulator screen. A box that looks like a keyboard will open. Click on "D0" in the stimulus window and then on "A" in the keyboard window. Then click on "D2" and then "S" in the keyboard window. Continue until all input signals are driven except for CLK.
To stimulate the clock, select the CLK signal from the list and then click on the "B_C: 0" button below the "0" in the stimulus dialog box as shown below. Then click on "SimGlobalReset" and then on the keyboard click on "R". We can now drive the D0-D3, the CLK, and the global reset. Pressing the "R" key will toggle the reset.

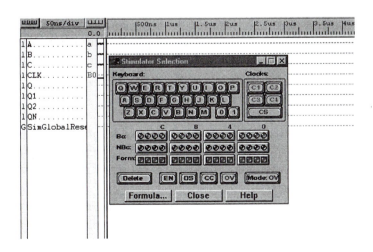

Step 4:

Toggle the "R" and the "CTRL". Next click on the "footsteps" icon in the menu bar at the top of the screen. Verify that the outputs follow the truth tables in the text.

Step 5:

You can perform a timing simulation of this same design by simply changing the pull-down menu in the menu bar from "Functional" to "Timing".

Now you can physically verify this design by downloading and testing it as in the "Quick Start OR-Gate lab."

Downloading and Testing Your Design

Step 6:

The next step is to download the design to the board as in the "Quick Start OR-Gate lab."

Step 7:

To test the design, use the switches on the board and observe the LEDs. Refer to your lab book to verify which pins are connected to the switches and LEDs.

Step 8:

Explain why the circuit of Figure 1 is called a decade counter.

_____

_____

_____

_____

Step 9:

Give a brief explanation of how the circuit works.

_____

_____

_____

_____

Experiment 48 Synchronous Binary Up-Counter Lab

Introduction

The purpose of this lab is to build, simulate and download a counter circuit using the Xilinx Foundation tools and Digilab Spartan board.

Objectives

After completing this lab, students will be able to:
- Demonstrate the operation of the circuit described.
- Perform a simple functional and timing simulation using the integrated simulation tool.

Preliminary Procedure

Follow the same steps as in the "Quick Start OR-Gate lab" to set up the lab board.

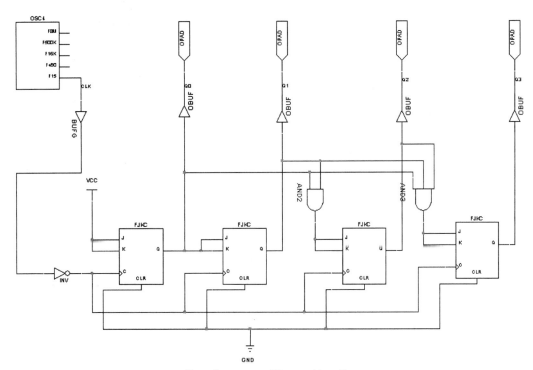

Synchronous Binary Up-Counter

Figure 1

241

Procedure

Create a new design with the Xilinx Foundation Series Schematic and name the design SBUP. You want to create a design that looks like Figure 1. Use the pin mapping sheet for the specific board you are using to select pins for the inputs and outputs of the design.

1) Once you finish creating the desired schematic, make sure to save it. <u>Click</u> **File → Save**. Then return to the Foundation Project Manager (press **<Alt>** + **<Tab>** to task switch).

2) The design entry is finished.

3) Next you need to implement the design the same way as in the Quick Start OR-Gate lab.

4) Click on the Implementation icon in the Project Manager window and follow the same procedure as in previous labs.

Activity Sheet Experiment 48
Synchronous Binary Up-Counter Lab

Name: _____

Date: _____

Using the Simulator

Step 1:
To simulate the operation of the circuits, first click on the SIM icon in the menu bar at the top of the schematic screen. The Logic Simulator will open.

Step 2:
Next, click on Signal -> Add Signals in the menu bar at the top of the simulator screen. Here you can decide which signals to drive and observe during the simulation. Note that the signals available are CLK, as well as the outputs Q0-Q3 (from the schematic), and SimGlobalReset. Recall that what SimGlobalReset does is to simulate a global reset on the PLD. It is always a good idea to use this initially just to ensure that you have a totally reset simulation before you start to drive signals.
Double-click on all of the signals (there will be a red checkmark to indicate selection). Then click on CLOSE at the bottom of the screen.

Step 3:
Now click on Signals -> Add Stimulators in the menu bar at the top of the simulator screen. A box that looks like a keyboard will open.
To stimulate the clock select the CLK signal from the list and then click on the "B_C: 0" button below the "0" in the stimulus dialog box as shown below. Then click on "SimGlobalReset" and then on the keyboard click on "R". We can now drive the CTRL, the CLK, and the global reset. Pressing the "R" key will toggle the reset.

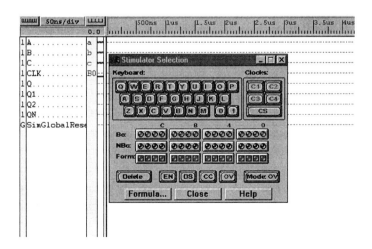

Step 4:
Toggle the "R" and the "CTRL". Next click on the "footsteps" icon in the menu bar at the top of the screen. Verify that the outputs follow the truth tables in the text.

Step 5:
You can perform a timing simulation of this same design by simply changing the pull-down menu in the menu bar from "Functional" to "Timing". Now you can physically verify this design by downloading and testing it as in the "Quickstart OR-Gate lab."

Downloading and Testing Your Design

Step 6:
Download the design to the board as in the "Quickstart OR-Gate lab."

Step 7:
To test the design, use the switches on the board and observe the LEDs. Refer to your lab book to verify which pins are connected to the switches and LEDs.

Step 8:
Give a brief explanation of the term *synchronous*.

_____

_____

_____

_____

Step 9:
Give a brief explanation of how the circuit works.

_____

_____

_____

_____

Experiment 49 Cascaded Counter Lab

Introduction

The purpose of this lab is to build, simulate, and download a counter circuit using the Xilinx Foundation tools and Digilab Spartan board.

Objectives

After completing this lab, students will be able to:

- Demonstrate the operation of the circuit described.
- Perform a simple functional and timing simulation using the integrated simulation tool.

Preliminary Procedure

Follow the same steps as in the "Quick Start OR-Gate lab" to set up the lab board.

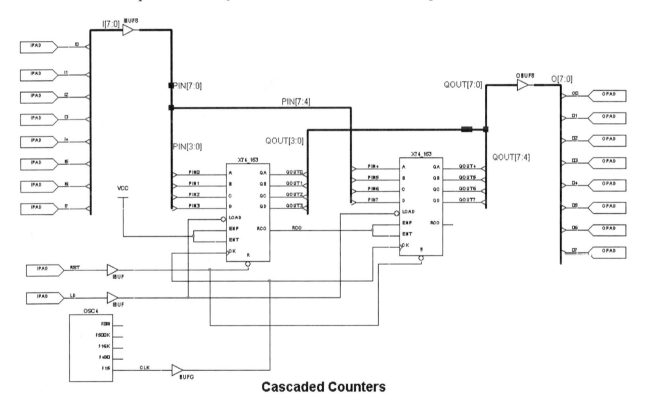

Cascaded Counters

Figure 1

Procedure

Create a new design with the Xilinx Foundation Series Schematic and name the design BCAS. You want to create a design that looks like Figure 1. Use the pin mapping sheet for the specific board you are using to select pins for the inputs and outputs of the design.

1) To connect the preset inputs and the outputs to the symbols and wires this schematic uses "busses." These are simply a way of drawing several wires as one, and they save a lot of time if you need more than 4 wires into a symbol that are all related, such as address or data lines. To draw a bus connection, use the Bus icon.

2) Then you have to name the bus, such that it has enough names (such as PIN0, PIN1, PIN2, etc.) to satisfy the number of wires that are being represented. You can do this by double-clicking on the bus itself and a window will open that already has the bus range (number of wires) on it and you will have to name it. In this case the input bus (after the IBUF) was named "PIN[7:0]. This is an 8-bit bus consisting of the preload input signals. You also need to name each separate wire that connects to the bus so that the software knows how to route and simulate the design.

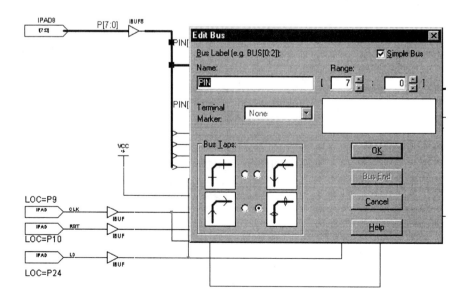

Cascaded Counters

246

3) Once you finish creating the desired schematic, make sure to save it. <u>Click</u> **File → Save**. Then return to the Foundation Project Manager (press **<Alt>** + **<Tab>** to task switch).

4) The design entry is finished.

5) Next you need to implement the design the same way as in the Quick Start OR-Gate lab.

6) Click on the Implementation icon in the Project Manager window and follow the same procedure as in previous labs.

Activity Sheet Experiment 49
Cascaded Counter Lab

Name: _____

Date: _____

Using the Simulator

Step 1:
To simulate the operation of the circuits, first click on the SIM icon in the menu bar at the top of the schematic screen. The Logic Simulator will open.

Step 2:
Next, click on Signal -> Add Signals in the menu bar at the top of the simulator screen. Here you can decide which signals to drive and observe during the simulation. Note that the signals available are P[7:0], RST, LD, and CLK, as well as the outputs Q[7:0] (from the schematic), and SimGlobalReset. Recall that what SimGlobalReset does is to simulate a global reset on the PLD. It is always a good idea to use this initially just to ensure that you have a totally reset simulation before you start to drive signals.
Double-click on all of the signals (there will be a red checkmark to indicate selection).
To "flatten" the bus signal so that you can drive each wire separately, select the bus name, right click on the signal, and then select Bus>Flatten. Then click on CLOSE at the bottom of the screen.

Step 3:
Now click on Signals -> Add Stimulators in the menu bar at the top of the simulator screen. A box that looks like a keyboard will open.
To stimulate the clock select the CLK signal from the list and then click on the "B$_C$: 0" button below the "0" in the stimulus dialog box as shown below. Then click on "SimGlobalReset" and then on the keyboard click on "R". We can now drive the CTRL, the CLK, and the global reset. Pressing the "R" key will toggle the reset.

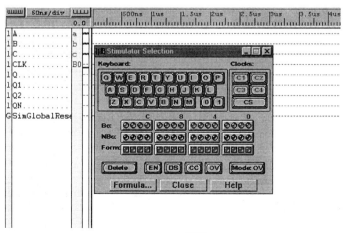

Step 4:

Toggle the "R" and the "CTRL". Next click on the "footsteps" icon in the menu bar at the top of the screen. Verify that the outputs follow the truth tables in the text.

Step 5:

You can perform a timing simulation of this same design by simply changing the pull-down menu in the menu bar from "Functional" to "Timing". Now you can physically verify this design by downloading and testing it as in the "Quick Start OR-Gate lab."

Downloading and Testing Your Design

Step 6:

Download the design to the board as in the "Quick Start OR-gate lab."

Step 7:

To test the design, use the switches on the board and observe the LEDs. Refer to your lab book to verify which pins are connected to the switches and LEDs.

Step 8:

Give a brief explanation of how the circuit works.

_____

_____

_____

_____

Experiment 50 N-Bit Counter Lab

Introduction

The purpose of this lab is to build, simulate, and download a counter circuit using the Xilinx Foundation tools and Digilab Spartan board.

Objectives

After completing this lab, students will be able to:
- Demonstrate the operation of the circuit described.
- Perform a simple functional and timing simulation using the integrated simulation tool

Preliminary Procedure

Follow the same steps as in the "Quick Start OR-Gate lab" to set up the lab board.

Procedure

Create a new design with the Xilinx Foundation Series Schematic and name the design NBIT. You want to create a design that looks like Figure 1. Use the board pin mapping sheet to select pins for the inputs and outputs of the design.

1) Once you finish creating the desired schematic, make sure to save it. <u>Click</u> **File → Save**. Then return to the Foundation Project Manager (press **<Alt> + <Tab>** to task switch).

2) The design entry is finished.

3) Next you need to implement the design the same way as in the Quick Start OR-Gate lab.

4) Click on the Implementation icon in the Project Manager window and follow the same procedure as in previous labs.

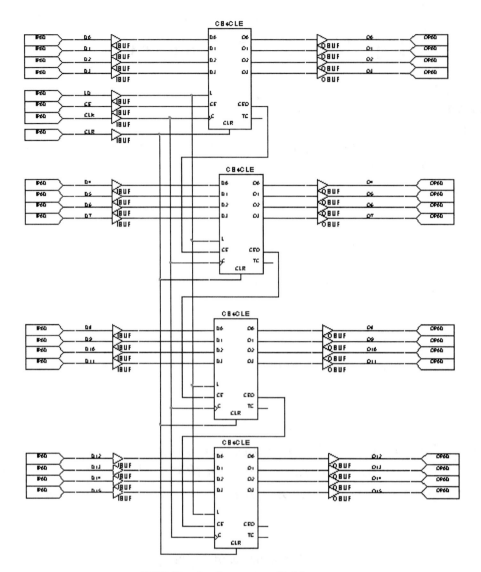

N-Bit Counter/Frequency Divider

Figure 1

HDL Alternative

Here is the code for the lab in VDHL. Follow the design flow in the "Using Hardware Design Languages (HDLs) with Xilinx tools" tutorial.

```vhdl
library IEEE;
  use IEEE.std_logic_1164.all;
  use IEEE.std_logic_unsigned.all;
  use IEEE.std_logic_arith.all;

  entity nbit is
    port (
      D: in STD_LOGIC_VECTOR (7 downto 0);
      LD: in STD_LOGIC;
      CLK: in STD_LOGIC;
      CLR: in STD_LOGIC;
      O: out STD_LOGIC_VECTOR (7 downto 0)
    );
  end nbit;

  architecture rtl of nbit is
    signal count: integer range 0 to 255;      -- Signal holds count
    signal count_to: integer range 0 to 255;   -- Signal holds the count to
  begin                                         -- Both have range constraints
    ld_and_count: process(CLK, CLR)             -- on the integer type
    begin
      if (CLR = '1') then  -- Reset the counter if CLR = '1'
        count <= 0;
      elsif (CLK'event and CLK='1') then      -- Perform on rising edge clock
        if (LD = '1') then                -- Either load the counter
          count_to <= CONV_INTEGER(D);
        else                              -- or count until count_to
          if (count = count_to) then      -- has been reached and then
            count <= 0;                   -- roll the count over
          else
            count <= count + 1;
          end if;
        end if;
      end if;
    end process ld_and_count;

  O <= CONV_STD_LOGIC_VECTOR(count, 8);       -- Convert the integer count
  end rtl;                                      -- to an 8-bit std_logic_vector
```

Here is the same lab using the Verilog HDL:

```verilog
module nbit (D, LD, CLK, CLR, O);
    input [7:0] D;
    input LD;
    input CLK;
    input CLR;
    output [7:0] O;

    reg [7:0] O;
    reg [7:0] count;      // the count value
    reg [7:0] count_to;   // the value we want to count to

    always @(posedge CLK or posedge CLR)  // Run always on positive edge
        begin: ld_and_count              // of CLK or CLR
        if (CLR == 1)
            count = 0;               // reset the count if CLR is high
        else
            if (LD == 1)
                count_to = D;        // load count_to value on clock
            else                     // edge and if LD is high
                if (count == count_to) // reset count if the count
                    count = 0;       // is equal to the count_to
                else
                    count = count + 1; // otherwise increment
    end

    always @(count)
        begin: assign_output
            O = count;               // assign the output of
        end                          // count to O
endmodule
```

Activity Sheet Experiment 50
N-Bit Counter Lab

Name: _____

Date: _____

Using the Simulator

Step 1:
To simulate the operation of the circuits first click on the SIM icon in the menu bar at the top of the schematic screen. The Logic Simulator will open.

Step 2:
Next, click on Signal -> Add Signals in the menu bar at the top of the simulator screen. Here you can decide which signals to drive and observe during the simulation. Note that the signals available are D0-D15, CE, LD, CLR, and CLK, as well as the outputs Q0-Q15 (from the schematic), and SimGlobalReset. Recall that what SimGlobalReset does is to simulate a global reset on the PLD. It is always a good idea to use this initially just to ensure that you have a totally reset simulation before you start to drive signals.
Double-click on all of the signals (there will be a red checkmark to indicate selection). Then click on CLOSE at the bottom of the screen.

Step 3:
Now click on Signals -> Add Stimulators in the menu bar at the top of the simulator screen. A box that looks like a keyboard will open. Click on "DO" in the stimulus window and select "A" from the keyboard screen. Next select "D1" from the stimulus window and click on "S" on the keyboard screen. Continue this process until you have selected all input signals except CLK.
To stimulate the clock, select the CLK signal from the list and then click on the "B_C: 0" button below the "0" in the stimulus dialog box as shown below. Then click on "SimGlobalReset" and then on the keyboard click on "R". We can now drive the CTRL, the CLK, and the global reset. Pressing the "R" key will toggle the reset.

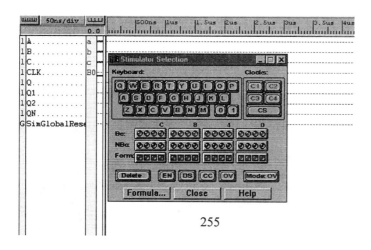

Step 4:
Toggle the "R" and the input signals. Next click on the "footsteps" icon in the menu bar at the top of the screen. Verify that the outputs follow the truth tables in the text.

Step 5:
You can perform a timing simulation of this same design by simply changing the pull-down menu in the menu bar from "Functional" to "Timing".

Now you can physically verify this design by downloading and testing it as in the "Quick Start OR-Gate lab."

Downloading and Testing Your Design

Step 6:
Download the design to the board as in the "Quick Start OR-Gate lab."

Step 7:
To test the design, use the switches on the board and observe the LEDs. Refer to your lab book to verify which pins are connected to the switches and LEDs.

Step 8:
Explain why this counter can also be termed a *frequency divider*.

_____

_____

_____

_____

Step 9:
Give a brief explanation of how the circuit works.

_____

_____

_____

_____

Experiment 51 Flasher Circuit Lab

Introduction

The purpose of this lab is to build, simulate, and download an up/down flasher circuit using the Xilinx Foundation tools and Digilab Spartan board.

Objectives

After completing this lab, students will be able to:
- Demonstrate the truth-table operation of an up/down counter.
- Perform a functional simulation of the flasher circuit using the integrated simulation tool.

Preliminary Procedure

Follow the same steps as in the "Quick Start OR-Gate lab" to set up the lab board.

Procedure

Create a new design with the Xilinx Foundation Series Schematic and name the design UDFLASH. You want to create a design that looks like Figure 1:

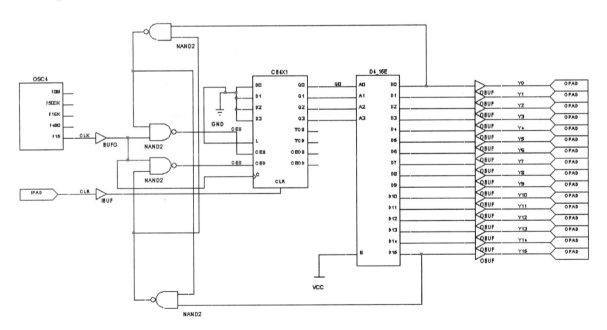

Up/Down Flasher Circuit
Figure 1

1) Once you finish creating the desired schematic, make sure to save it. <u>Click</u> **File → Save**. Ensure that you have locked pins according to the board you are using. See appendix for common board pinouts. Then return to the Foundation Project Manager (press **<Alt>** + **<Tab>** to task switch).

2) The design entry is finished.

Activity Sheet Experiment 51
Flasher Circuit Lab

Name: _____

Date: _____

Using the Simulator

Step 1:
This is another chance to practice with the Aldec™ logic simulation tool integrated with the Xilinx software. To simulate the operation of the decoders, first click on the SIM icon in the menu bar at the top of the schematic screen. The Logic Simulator will open.

Step 2:
Next, click on Signal -> Add Signals in the menu bar at the top of the simulator screen. Here you can decide which signals to drive and observe during the simulation. Note that the signals available are only CLK and CLR, as well as the 16 outputs: Y0-Y15 (from the schematic), and something called SimGlobalReset. Recall that what SimGlobalReset does is to simulate a global reset on the PLD. It is always a good idea to use this initially just to ensure that you have a totally reset simulation before you start to drive signals.
Double-click on all of the signals (there will be a red checkmark to indicate selection). Then click on CLOSE at the bottom of the screen.

Step 3:
Now click on Signals -> Add Stimulators in the menu bar at the top of the simulator screen. A box that looks like a keyboard will open. Click on the signal "CLR" in the upper-left portion of the screen and then on the "C" on the keyboard (on the screen). Next click on CLK in the signal list and then on the oval under the red zero on the Bc: line in the stimulator box. Then click on "SimGlobalReset" and then on the keyboard click on "R". We can now drive the inputs and the global reset. Pressing the "R" key will toggle the reset and pressing the "C" key will toggle the "CLR" input to the counter.

Step 4:
Toggle the "R" and the clear signals and then click on the "footsteps" in the menu bar at the top of the screen. You should be able to see the counter counting up and then down.
Hint: Move the signals Y0, Y1, Y2, etc. under each other so that you are able to see the "ripple" effect of the counter. You can easily do this by holding the left mouse button down over the signal to be moved and releasing it when you have it where you want it in the list.

Now you can physically verify this design by implementing it as in the "Quick Start OR-Gate lab."

Downloading and Testing Your Design

Step 5:
Download the design to the board as in the "Quick Start OR-Gate lab."

Step 6:
To test the Back and Forth Flasher design use the switch on the board to drive "CLR" low and observe the LEDs and on the 7-segment LEDs. Since there are only eight segments in the LED bar, we have also used the 7-segment LEDs for the other eight signals. Refer to your lab book to verify which pins are connected to which LED segments.

Step 7:
Give a brief explanation of how the circuit works.

_____

_____

_____

_____

Experiment 52 Stopwatch Lab

Introduction

The purpose of this lab is to simulate and download a stopwatch circuit using the Xilinx Foundation tools and Digilab Spartan board.

Objectives

After completing this lab, students will be able to:

- Demonstrate the operation of the design described.
- Perform a simple functional and timing simulation using the integrated simulation tool.

Preliminary Procedure

Follow the same steps as in the "Quick Start OR-Gate lab" to set up the lab board.

Procedure

Load a tutorial project from the Xilinx Foundation Series called WATCHNEW. The design looks like Figure 1:

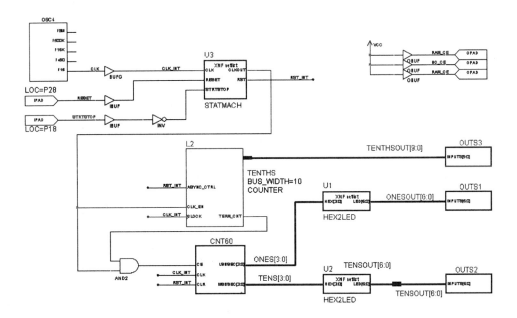

Figure 1

2) This design is a stopwatch. You can use the Hierarchy icon to look down into these modules, such as CNT60 and STAMACH, to see how they were designed. Ensure that you have locked pins according to the board you are using. See the appendix for common board pinouts.

3) The design entry has been finished for you (except for the pin locking).

4) Next you need to implement the design the same way as in the Quick Start OR-Gate lab.

5) Click on the Implementation icon in the Project Manager window and follow the same procedure as in previous labs.

Activity Sheet Experiment 52
Stopwatch Lab

Name: _____

Date: _____

Using the Simulator

Step 1:
To simulate the operation of the Watchnew, first click on the SIM icon in the menu bar at the top of the schematic screen. The Logic Simulator will open.

Step 2:
Next, click on Signal -> Add Signals in the menu bar at the top of the simulator screen. Here you can decide which signals to drive and observe during the simulation. Note that the signals available are RESET STARTSTOP and CLK, as well as the outputs: OUTS1, OUTS2, and OUTS3 (from the schematic), and something called SimGlobalReset. Recall that what SimGlobalReset does is to simulate a global reset on the PLD. It is always a good idea to use this initially just to ensure that you have a totally reset simulation before you start to drive signals.
Double-click on all of the signals (there will be a red checkmark to indicate selection). Then click on CLOSE at the bottom of the screen.

Step 3:
Now click on Signals -> Add Stimulators in the menu bar at the top of the simulator screen. A box that looks like a keyboard will open. Click on the signal "STARTSTOP" in the upper left portion of the screen and then on the "Q" on the keyboard (on the screen). Do the same for RESET using the letter "S". Set up the CLK signal as in previous labs using the "Bc:" line in the keyboard screen.
Then click on "SimGlobalReset" and then on the keyboard click on "R". We can now drive the inputs and the global reset. Pressing the "R" key will toggle the reset and pressing the "Q" key will toggle the "STARTSTOP" input to the circuit, and so on.

Step 4:
Toggle the "R" and the input signals and then click on the "footsteps" in the menu bar at the top of the screen. Verify that the circuit works using the truth table provided in the text.

Step 5:
You can perform a timing simulation of this same design by simply changing the pull-down menu in the menu bar from "Functional" to "Timing".

Now you can physically verify this design by downloading and testing it as in the "Quick Start OR-Gate lab."

Downloading and Testing Your Design

Step 6:
Download the design to the board as in the "Quick Start OR-gate lab."

Step 7:
To test the design, use the switches on the board and observe the LEDs. Refer to your lab book to verify which pins are connected to the switches and LEDs.

Step 8:
What is the name of the design language used in the "HEX2LED" modules?

_____

_____

_____

_____

Step 9:
Give a brief explanation of how the circuit works.

_____

_____

_____

_____

Experiment 53 Half-Adder Lab

Introduction

The purpose of this lab is to build, simulate, and download a half-adder circuit using the Xilinx Foundation tools and Digilab Spartan board.

Objectives

After completing this lab, students will be able to:
- Demonstrate the operation of the half-adder described.
- Perform a simple functional and timing simulation using the integrated simulation tool.

Preliminary Procedure

Follow the same steps as in the "Quick Start OR-Gate lab" to set up the lab board.

Procedure

Create a new design with the Xilinx Foundation Series Schematic and name the design HADDER. You want to create a design that looks like Figure 1:

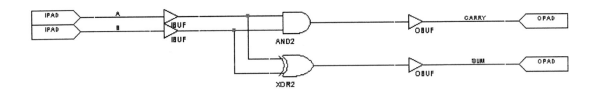

Half Adder (HA)

Figure 1

1) Once you finish creating the desired schematic, make sure to save it. <u>Click</u> **File → Save**. Ensure that you have locked pins according to the board you are using. See the appendix for common board pinouts. Then return to the Foundation Project Manager (press **<Alt>** + **<Tab>** to task switch).

2) The design entry is finished.

3) Next you need to implement the design the same way as in the Quick Start OR-Gate lab.

4) Click on the Implementation icon in the Project Manager window and follow the same procedure as in previous labs.

Activity Sheet Experiment 53
Half-Adder Lab

Name: _____

Date: _____

Using the Simulator

Step 1:
To simulate the operation of the half-adder, first click on the SIM icon in the menu bar at the top of the schematic screen. The Logic Simulator will open.

Step 2:
Next, click on Signal -> Add Signals in the menu bar at the top of the simulator screen. Here you can decide which signals to drive and observe during the simulation. Note that the signals available are A and B, as well as the outputs: CARRY and SUM (from the schematic), and something called SimGlobalReset. Recall that what SimGlobalReset does is to simulate a global reset on the PLD. It is always a good idea to use this initially just to ensure that you have a totally reset simulation before you start to drive signals.
Double-click on all of the signals (there will be a red checkmark to indicate selection). Then click on CLOSE at the bottom of the screen.

Step 3:
Now click on Signals -> Add Stimulators in the menu bar at the top of the simulator screen. A box that looks like a keyboard will open. Click on the signal "A" in the upper-left portion of the screen and then on the "A" on the keyboard (on the screen). Do the same for B using the letter "S". Then click on "SimGlobalReset" and then on the keyboard click on "R" We can now drive the inputs and the global reset. Pressing the "R" key will toggle the reset and pressing the "A" key will toggle the "A" input to the half-adder, and so on.

Step 4:
Toggle the "R" and the input signals and then click on the "footsteps" in the menu bar at the top of the screen. Complete the following truth table:

A	B	SUM	CARRY
0	0		
0	1		
1	0		
1	1		

Step 5:

You can perform a timing simulation of this same design by simply changing the pull-down menu in the menu bar from "Functional" to "Timing".

Now you can physically verify this design by downloading and testing it as in the "Quick Start OR-Gate lab."

Downloading and Testing Your Design

Step 6:

Download the design to the board as in the "Quick Start OR-gate lab."

Step 7:

To test the design, use the switches on the board and observe the LEDs. Refer to your lab book to verify which pins are connected to the switches and LEDs.

Step 8:

Give a brief explanation of how the circuit works.

_____

_____

_____

_____

Experiment 54 Full-Adder Lab

Introduction

The purpose of this lab is to build, simulate, and download a full-adder circuit using the Xilinx Foundation tools and Digilab Spartan board.

Objectives

After completing this lab, students will be able to:
- Demonstrate the operation of the full-adder described.
- Perform a simple functional and timing simulation using the integrated simulation tool.

Preliminary Procedure

Follow the same steps as in the "Quick Start OR-Gate lab" to set up the lab board.

Procedure

Create a new design with the Xilinx Foundation Series Schematic and name the design FADDER. You want to create a design that looks like Figure 1:

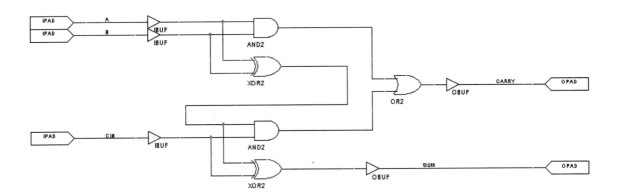

Full Adder (FA)

Figure 1

1) Once you finish creating the desired schematic, make sure to save it. <u>Click</u> **File → Save**. Ensure that you have locked pins according to the board you are using. See the appendix for common board pinouts. Then return to the Foundation Project Manager (press **<Alt>** + **<Tab>** to task switch).

2) The design entry is finished.

3) Next you need to implement the design the same way as in the Quick Start OR-Gate lab.

4) Click on the Implementation icon in the Project Manager window and follow the same procedure as in previous labs.

HDL Alternative

Here is the code for the lab in VDHL. Follow the design flow in the "Using Hardware Design Languages (HDLs) with Xilinx tools" tutorial.

```
library IEEE;
use IEEE.std_logic_1164.all;

entity fadder is
  port (
    A: in STD_LOGIC;
    B: in STD_LOGIC;
    CIN: in STD_LOGIC;
    COUT: out STD_LOGIC;
    SUM: out STD_LOGIC
  );
end fadder;

architecture rtl of fadder is
begin
    COUT <= (A and B) or (B and CIN) or (A and CIN);     -- K-map equations for
    SUM <= A xor B xor CIN;                              -- carry out and sum
end rtl;
```

And here is the lab project again, this time using the Verilog design language:

```
module fadder (A, B, CIN, COUT, SUM);
  input A;
  input B;
  input CIN;
  output COUT;
  output SUM;

  reg COUT;
  reg SUM;

  always @(A or B or CIN)  // Assign the k-map equations in always
    begin: fa           // block and run whenever A, B, or CIN changes
      COUT = (A & B) | (B & CIN) | (A & CIN);
      SUM = A ^ B ^ CIN;
    end
endmodule
```

Activity Sheet Experiment 54
Full-Adder Lab

Name: _____

Date: _____

Using the Simulator

Step 1:
To simulate the operation of the full-adder, first click on the SIM icon in the menu bar at the top of the schematic screen. The Logic Simulator will open.

Step 2:
Next, click on Signal -> Add Signals in the menu bar at the top of the simulator screen. Here you can decide which signals to drive and observe during the simulation. Note that the signals available are CIN, A, and B, as well as the outputs: CARRY and SUM (from the schematic), and something called SimGlobalReset. Recall that what SimGlobalReset does is to simulate a global reset on the PLD. It is always a good idea to use this initially just to ensure that you have a totally reset simulation before you start to drive signals.
Double-click on all of the signals (there will be a red checkmark to indicate selection). Then click on CLOSE at the bottom of the screen.

Step 3:
Now click on Signals -> Add Stimulators in the menu bar at the top of the simulator screen. A box that looks like a keyboard will open. Click on the signal "A" in the upper left portion of the screen and then on the "A" on the keyboard (on the screen). Do the same for B using the letter "S" and with CIN using the letter "D". Then click on "SimGlobalReset" and then on the keyboard click on "R". We can now drive the inputs and the global reset. Pressing the "R" key will toggle the reset and pressing the "A" key will toggle the "A" input to the full-adder, and so on.

Step 4:
Toggle the "R" and the input signals and then click on the "footsteps" in the menu bar at the top of the screen. Verify that the following truth table is valid:

CIN	A	B	SUM	CARRY
0	0	0		
0	0	1		
0	1	0		
0	1	1		
1	0	0		
1	0	1		
1	1	0		
1	1	1		

Step 5:
You can perform a timing simulation of this same design by simply changing the pull-down menu in the menu bar from "Functional" to "Timing".

Now you can physically verify this design by downloading and testing it as in the "Quick Start OR-Gate lab."

Downloading and Testing Your Design

Step 6:
Download the design to the board as in the "Quick Start OR-gate lab."

Step 7:
To test the design, use the switches on the board and observe the LEDs. Refer to your lab book to verify which pins are connected to the switches and LEDs.

Step 8:
Give a brief explanation of the difference between a half-adder and a full-adder.

_____

_____

_____

_____

Step 9:
Give a brief explanation of how the full-adder circuit works.

_____

_____

_____

_____

Experiment 55 Parallel-Adder Lab

Introduction

The purpose of this lab is to build, simulate, and download a parallel 4-bit adder circuit using the Xilinx Foundation tools and Digilab Spartan board.

Objectives

After completing this lab, students will be able to:
- Demonstrate the operation of the 4-bit adder described.
- Perform a simple functional and timing simulation using the integrated simulation tool.

Preliminary Procedure

Follow the same steps as in the "Quick Start OR-Gate lab" to set up the lab board.

Procedure

Create a new design with the Xilinx Foundation Series Schematic and name the design PADDER. You want to create a design that looks like Figure 1:

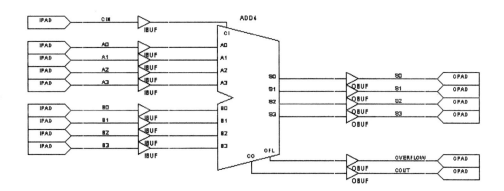

Parallel Adder

Figure 1

1) Once you finish creating the desired schematic, make sure to save it. Click **File → Save**. Ensure that you have locked pins according to the board you are using. See the appendix for common board pinouts. Then return to the Foundation Project Manager (press **<Alt> + <Tab>** to task switch). Note: Be sure to name the busses as in previous labs where bussing was used or the circuit will not simulate properly.

2) The design entry is finished.

3) To see how the adder is actually built, click on the "H" Hierarchy icon on the left side of the screen, and then click on the add4 component. You will be "pushed" down a hierarchy level. To get back to the top level schematic, right-click and select "Hierarchy Pop" from the menu.

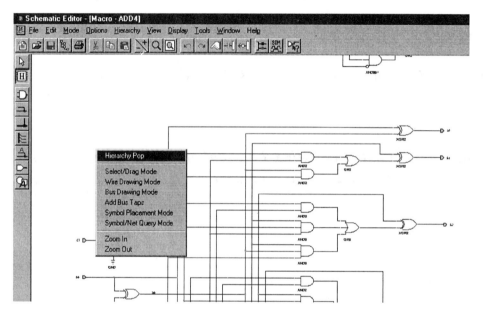

4) Next you need to implement the design the same way as in the Quick Start OR-Gate lab.

5) Click on the Implementation icon in the Project Manager window and follow the same procedure as in previous labs.

Activity Sheet Experiment 55
Parallel-Adder Lab

Name: _____

Date: _____

Using the Simulator

Step 1:
To simulate the operation of the 8-bit adder, first click on the SIM icon in the menu bar at the top of the schematic screen. The Logic Simulator will open.

Step 2:
Next, click on Signal -> Add Signals in the menu bar at the top of the simulator screen. Here you can decide which signals to drive and observe during the simulation. Note that the signals available are CIN, A0-A3, and B0-B3, as well as the outputs: S0-S3, Overflow, and Carry (from the schematic), and something called SimGlobalReset. Recall that what SimGlobalReset does is to simulate a global reset on the PLD. It is always a good idea to use this initially just to ensure that you have a totally reset simulation before you start to drive signals.
Double-click on all of the signals (there will be a red checkmark to indicate selection). Then click on CLOSE at the bottom of the screen.

Step 3:
Now click on Signals -> Add Stimulators in the menu bar at the top of the simulator screen. A box that looks like a keyboard will open. Click on the signal "A0" in the upper-left portion of the screen and then on the "A" on the keyboard (on the screen). Do the same for A1 using the letter "S" and with A2-3, B-3, and CIN using other letters on the keyboard screen. Then click on "SimGlobalReset" and then on the keyboard click on "R". We can now drive the inputs and the global reset. Pressing the "R" key will toggle the reset and pressing the "A" key will toggle the "A0" input to the adder, and so on.

Step 4:
Toggle the "R" and the input signals and then click on the "footsteps" in the menu bar at the top of the screen. Verify that the circuit works using the truth table provided in the text.

Step 5:
You can perform a timing simulation of this same design by simply changing the pull-down menu in the menu bar from "Functional" to "Timing".

Now you can physically verify this design by downloading and testing it as in the "Quick Start OR-Gate lab."

Downloading and Testing Your Design

Step 6:
Download the design to the board as in the "Quick Start OR-Gate lab."

Step 7:
To test the design, use the switches on the board and observe the LEDs. Refer to your lab book to verify which pins are connected to the switches and LEDs.

Step 8:
Give a brief explanation of how the parallel-adder circuit works.

_____

_____

_____

_____

Experiment 56 8-Bit Parallel-Adder Lab

Introduction

The purpose of this lab is to build, simulate, and download a parallel 8-bit adder circuit using the Xilinx Foundation tools and Digilab Spartan board.

Objectives

After completing this lab, students will be able to:
- Demonstrate the operation of the basic 8-bit adder described.
- Perform a simple functional and timing simulation using the integrated simulation tool.

Preliminary Procedure

Follow the same steps as in the "Quick Start OR-Gate lab" to set up the lab board.

Procedure

Create a new design with the Xilinx Foundation Series Schematic and name the design PADD8. You want to create a design that looks like Figure 1:

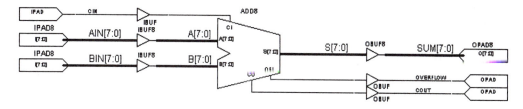

8-Bit Parallel Adder

Figure 1

1) Once you finish creating the desired schematic, make sure to save it. <u>Click</u> **File → Save**. Ensure that you have locked pins according to the board you are using. See the appendix for common board pinouts.

2) Then return to the Foundation Project Manager (press **<Alt> + <Tab>** to task switch). Note: Be sure to name the busses as in previous labs where bussing was used or the circuit will not simulate properly.

3) The design entry is finished.

4) To see how the adder is actually built, click on the "H" Hierarchy icon on the left side of the screen, then click on the add8 component. You will be "pushed" down a hierarchy level. Click again on the add4X2 component. To get back to the top level schematic, right click, and select "Hierarchy Pop" twice from the menu.

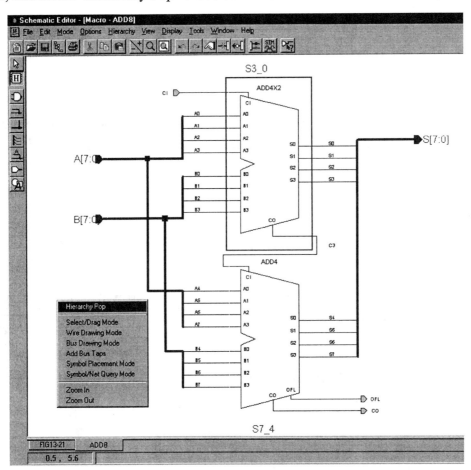

Question: How do you get down to the gate level in this macro? Hint: There are several levels of hierarchy.

5) Next you need to implement the design the same way as in the Quick Start OR-Gate lab.

6) Click on the Implementation icon in the Project Manager window and follow the same procedure as in previous labs.

HDL Alternative

Here is the code for the lab in VDHL. Follow the design flow in the "Using Hardware Design Languages (HDLs) with Xilinx tools" tutorial.
This design consists of two files. Name the first padd4.vhd. Here is the code for that file:

```vhdl
library IEEE;
use IEEE.std_logic_1164.all;

entity padd4 is
    port (
        CIN: in STD_LOGIC;
        AIN: in STD_LOGIC_VECTOR (3 downto 0);-- 4-bit A operand
        BIN: in STD_LOGIC_VECTOR (3 downto 0);-- 4-bit B operand
        SUM: out STD_LOGIC_VECTOR (3 downto 0);        -- Output sum
        COUT: out STD_LOGIC;                    -- Carry out
        OVERFLOW: out STD_LOGIC                  -- Overflow
    );
end padd4;

architecture rtl of padd4 is
    component fadder                    -- Full adder component
        port (
            A: in STD_LOGIC;
            B: in STD_LOGIC;
            CIN: in STD_LOGIC;
            COUT: out STD_LOGIC;
            SUM: out STD_LOGIC
        );
    end component;

    signal carry: STD_LOGIC_VECTOR(3 downto 0);        -- Carry propagate signal
begin
    fadder_0: fadder                    -- Full adder components (0 to 3)
        port map (AIN(0), BIN(0), CIN, carry(0), SUM(0));

    fadder_1: fadder
        port map (AIN(1), BIN(1), carry(0), carry(1), SUM(1));

    fadder_2: fadder
        port map (AIN(2), BIN(2), carry(1), carry(2), SUM(2));

    fadder_3: fadder
        port map (AIN(3), BIN(3), carry(2), carry(3), SUM(3));
```

```
COUT <= carry(3);                          -- Output carry (=carry(3))
OVERFLOW <= carry(2) xor carry(3);         -- Overflow (=carry-in (msb) xor'd
end rtl;                                   -- with carry-out (msb))
```

The second file should be called fadder.vhd. Here is the code for that file:

```
library IEEE;
use IEEE.std_logic_1164.all;

entity fadder is
  port (
    A: in STD_LOGIC;
    B: in STD_LOGIC;
    CIN: in STD_LOGIC;
    COUT: out STD_LOGIC;
    SUM: out STD_LOGIC
  );
end fadder;

architecture rtl of fadder is
begin
  COUT <= (A and B) or (B and CIN) or (A and CIN);    -- K-map equations for
  SUM <= A xor B xor CIN;                             -- carry out and sum
end rtl;
```

Here is the same function using the Verilog HDL. First the padd4.ver file:

```
module padd4 (CIN, AIN, BIN, SUM, COUT, OVERFLOW) ;
  input CIN;
  input [3:0] AIN;
  input [3:0] BIN;
  output [3:0] SUM;
  output COUT;
  output OVERFLOW;

  reg [3:0] SUM;
  reg COUT;
  reg OVERFLOW;
  reg [3:0] carry;

  fadder fadder_0(.A(AIN[0]), .B(BIN[0]), .CIN(CIN), .COUT(carry[0]), .SUM(SUM[0]));
  fadder fadder_1(.A(AIN[1]), .B(BIN[1]), .CIN(carry[0]), .COUT(carry[1]),
.SUM(SUM[1]));
  fadder fadder_2(.A(AIN[2]), .B(BIN[2]), .CIN(carry[1]), .COUT(carry[2]),
.SUM(SUM[2]));
```

```
      fadder fadder_3(.A(AIN[3]), .B(BIN[3]), .CIN(carry[2]), .COUT(carry[3]),
.SUM(SUM[3]));

   always @(carry)
      begin: cout_and_overflow
         COUT = carry[3];
         OVERFLOW = carry[2] ^ carry[3];
      end
endmodule
```

Here is the adder.ver file in Verilog HDL language:

```
module fadder (A, B, CIN, COUT, SUM);
   input A;
   input B;
   input CIN;
   output COUT;
   output SUM;

   reg COUT;
   reg SUM;

   always @(A or B or CIN)  // Assign the k-map equations in always
      begin: fa          // block and run whenever A, B, or CIN changes
         COUT = (A & B) | (B & CIN) | (A & CIN);
         SUM = A ^ B ^ CIN;
      end
                                        endmodule
```

Activity Sheet Experiment 56
8-Bit Parallel-Adder Lab

Name: _____

Date: _____

Using the Simulator

Step 1:
To simulate the operation of the 8-bit adder first click on the SIM icon in the menu bar at the top of the schematic screen. The Logic Simulator will open.

Step 2:
Next, click on Signal -> Add Signals in the menu bar at the top of the simulator screen. Here you can decide which signals to drive and observe during the simulation. Note that the signals available are C, A[7:0], and B[7:0], as well as the outputs: S[7:0] (from the schematic), and something called SimGlobalReset. Recall that what SimGlobalReset does is to simulate a global reset on the PLD. It is always a good idea to use this initially just to ensure that you have a totally reset simulation before you start to drive signals. Double-click on all of the signals (there will be a red checkmark to indicate selection). Then click on CLOSE at the bottom of the screen.

Step 3:
Select the bus signal A[7:0] and right-click. Then select Bus>Flatten to expand the bus to individual signals A0,A1,A2 etc. Do the same for the B bus.

Step 4:
Now click on Signals -> Add Stimulators in the menu bar at the top of the simulator screen. A box that looks like a keyboard will open. Click on the signal "AIN0" in the upper left portion of the screen and then on the "A" on the keyboard (on the screen). Do the same for A1 using the letter "S" and with A2-7, B0-7, and C using other letters on the keyboard screen. Then click on "SimGlobalReset" and then on the keyboard click on "R". We can now drive the inputs and the global reset. Pressing the "R" key will toggle the reset and pressing the "A" key will toggle the "A0" input to the adder, and so on.

Step 5:
Toggle the "R" and the input signals and then click on the "footsteps" in the menu bar at the top of the screen. Verify that the circuit works using the truth table provided in the text.

Step 6:
You can perform a timing simulation of this same design by simply changing the pull-down menu in the menu bar from "Functional" to "Timing".

Now you can physically verify this design by downloading and testing it as in the "Quick Start OR-Gate lab."

Downloading and Testing Your Design

Step 7:
Download the design to the board as in the "Quick Start OR-Gate lab."

Step 8:
To test the design, use the switches on the board and observe the LEDs. Refer to your lab book to verify which pins are connected to the switches and LEDs.

Step 9:
Give a brief explanation of how the 8-bit parallel adder circuit works.

_____

_____

_____

_____

Experiment 57 Adder/Subtractor Lab

Introduction

The purpose of this lab is to build, simulate, and download an 8-bit adder/subtractor circuit using the Xilinx Foundation tools and Digilab Spartan board.

Objectives

After completing this lab, students will be able to:
- Demonstrate the operation of the adder/subtractor described.
- Perform a simple functional and timing simulation using the integrated simulation tool.

Preliminary Procedure

Follow the same steps as in the "Quick Start OR-Gate lab" to set up the lab board.

Procedure

Create a new design with the Xilinx Foundation Series Schematic and name the design ADDSUB. Use the board pin mapping sheet to select pins for the inputs and outputs of the design.
You want to create a design that looks like Figure 1:

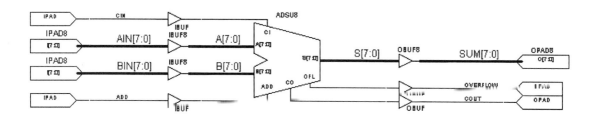

8-Bit Adder/Subtractor

Figure 1

1) Once you finish creating the schematic, make sure to save it. <u>Click</u> **File → Save**. Then return to the Foundation Project Manager (press **<Alt>** + **<Tab>** to task switch). Note: Be sure to name the busses as in previous labs where bussing was used or the circuit will not simulate properly.

2) The design entry is finished.

3) To see how the adder/subtractor is actually built, click on the "H" Hierarchy icon on the left side of the screen, then click on the adsu8 component. You will be "pushed" down a level. Click again on the adsu4X2 and again on the adsu2X1 component and you will be pushed down another level into the AND, OR, and XOR gates that actually make up the design. To get back to the top level schematic, right-click and select "Hierarchy Pop" three times from the menu.

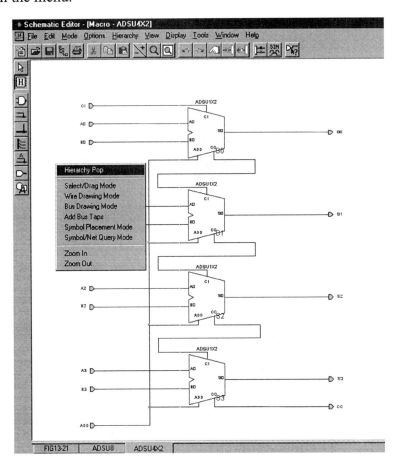

4) Next you need to implement the design the same way as in the Quick Start OR-Gate lab.

5) Click on the Implementation icon in the Project Manager window and follow the same procedure as in previous labs.

HDL Alternative

Here is the code for the lab in VDHL. Follow the design flow in the "Using Hardware Design Languages (HDLs) with Xilinx tools" tutorial. This design consists of two VHDL modules (files). This first one is called "addsub".

```
library IEEE;
use IEEE.std_logic_1164.all;

entity addsub is
   port (
      CIN: in STD_LOGIC;
      ADD: in STD_LOGIC;
      AIN: in STD_LOGIC_VECTOR (3 downto 0);-- 4-bit A operand
      BIN: in STD_LOGIC_VECTOR (3 downto 0);-- 4-bit B operand
      SUM: out STD_LOGIC_VECTOR (3 downto 0);      -- Output sum
      COUT: out STD_LOGIC;                    -- Carry out
      OVERFLOW: out STD_LOGIC                   -- Overflow
   );
end addsub;

architecture rtl of addsub is
   component fadder                      -- Full adder component
      port (
         A: in STD_LOGIC;
         B: in STD_LOGIC;
         CIN: in STD_LOGIC;
         COUT: out STD_LOGIC;
         SUM: out STD_LOGIC
      );
   end component;

   signal int_bin: STD_LOGIC_VECTOR(3 downto 0); -- Internal BIN signal
   signal int_cin: STD_LOGIC;                    -- Internal carry in signal
   signal carry: STD_LOGIC_VECTOR(3 downto 0);        -- Carry propagate signal
begin
   int_cin <= CIN when (ADD = '1') else '1'; -- These operation set the add
   int_bin <= BIN when (ADD = '1') else (not BIN);  -- or subtract (2's comp) mode

   fadder_0: fadder                      -- Full adder components (0 to 3)
      port map (AIN(0), int_bin(0), int_cin, carry(0), SUM(0));

   fadder_1: fadder
      port map (AIN(1), int_bin(1), carry(0), carry(1), SUM(1));

   fadder_2: fadder
```

```
    port map (AIN(2), int_bin(2), carry(1), carry(2), SUM(2));

  fadder_3: fadder
    port map (AIN(3), int_bin(3), carry(2), carry(3), SUM(3));

  COUT <= carry(3);                        -- Output carry (=carry(3))
  OVERFLOW <= carry(2) xor carry(3);       -- Overflow (=carry-in (msb) xor'd
end rtl;                                   -- with carry-out (msb))
```

This is the second VHDL module called "fadder". Can you figure out what it does?

```
library IEEE;
use IEEE.std_logic_1164.all;

entity fadder is
  port (
    A: in STD_LOGIC;
    B: in STD_LOGIC;
    CIN: in STD_LOGIC;
    COUT: out STD_LOGIC;
    SUM: out STD_LOGIC
  );
end fadder;

architecture rtl of fadder is
begin
  COUT <= (A and B) or (B and CIN) or (A and CIN);    -- K-map equations for
  SUM <= A xor B xor CIN;                             -- carry out and sum
end rtl;
```

And here is the lab project yet again this time using the Verilog design language:
This is also two files. The first module is called "addsub". Here is the code:

```
module addsub (CIN, ADD, AIN, BIN, SUM, COUT, OVERFLOW);
  input CIN;
  input ADD;
  input [3:0] AIN;
  input [3:0] BIN;
  output [3:0] SUM;
  output COUT;
  output OVERFLOW;

  reg [3:0] SUM;
  reg COUT;
  reg OVERFLOW;
```

```verilog
  reg [3:0] int_bin;
  reg int_cin;
  reg [3:0] carry;

  always @(ADD or CIN or BIN)
    begin: add_or_sub
      if (ADD == 1)
        begin
          int_cin = CIN;
          int_bin = BIN;
        end
      else if (ADD == 0)
        begin
          int_cin = 1'b 1;
          int_bin = ~BIN;
        end
    end

    fadder fadder_0(.A(AIN[0]), .B(int_bin[0]), .CIN(int_cin), .COUT(carry[0]),
.SUM(SUM[0]));
   fadder fadder_1(.A(AIN[1]), .B(int_bin[1]), .CIN(carry[0]), .COUT(carry[1]),
.SUM(SUM[1]));
   fadder fadder_2(.A(AIN[2]), .B(int_bin[2]), .CIN(carry[1]), .COUT(carry[2]),
.SUM(SUM[2]));
   fadder fadder_3(.A(AIN[3]), .B(int_bin[3]), .CIN(carry[2]), .COUT(carry[3]),
.SUM(SUM[3]));

  always @(carry)
    begin: cout_and_overflow
      COUT = carry[3];
      OVERFLOW = carry[2] ^ carry[3];
    end
endmodule
```

The second file is called "fadder" and this is the code for the full adder module in Verilog:

```verilog
module fadder (A, B, CIN, COUT, SUM);
  input A;
  input B;
  input CIN;
  output COUT;
  output SUM;

  reg COUT;
  reg SUM;
```

```
always @(A or B or CIN)  // Assign the k-map equations in always
   begin: fa          // block and run whenever A, B, or CIN changes
     COUT = (A & B) | (B & CIN) | (A & CIN);
     SUM = A ^ B ^ CIN;
   end
endmodule
```

Activity Sheet Experiment 57
Adder/Subtractor Lab

Name: _____

Date: _____

Using the Simulator

Step 1:
To simulate the operation of the 8-bit adder, first click on the SIM icon in the menu bar at the top of the schematic screen. The Logic Simulator will open.

Step 2:
Next, click on Signal -> Add Signals in the menu bar at the top of the simulator screen. Here you can decide which signals to drive and observe during the simulation. Note that the signals available are ADD, CIN, AIN[7:0], and BIN[7:0], as well as the outputs: SUM[7:0] (from the schematic), and something called SimGlobalReset. Recall that what SimGlobalReset does is to simulate a global reset on the PLD. It is always a good idea to use this initially just to ensure that you have a totally reset simulation before you start to drive signals.
Double-click on all of the signals (there will be a red checkmark to indicate selection). Then click on CLOSE at the bottom of the screen.

Step 3:
Select the bus signal AIN[7:0] and right-click. Then select Bus>Flatten to expand the bus to individual signals A0, A1, A2, etc. Do the same for the BIN bus.

Step 4:
Now click on Signals -> Add Stimulators in the menu bar at the top of the simulator screen. A box that looks like a keyboard will open. Click on the signal "AIN0" in the upper left portion of the screen and then on the "A" on the keyboard (on the screen). Do the same for AIN1using the letter "S" and with AIN2-7, BIN0-7, ADD, and CIN using other letters on the keyboard screen. Then click on "SimGlobalReset" and then on the keyboard click on "R". We can now drive the inputs and the global reset. Pressing the "R" key will toggle the reset and pressing the "A" key will toggle the "A0" input to the adder, and so on.

Step 5:
Toggle the "R" and the input signals and then click on the "footsteps" in the menu bar at the top of the screen. Verify that the circuit works using the truth table provided in the text.

Step 6:
You can perform a timing simulation of this same design by simply changing the pull-down menu in the menu bar from "Functional" to "Timing".

Now you can physically verify this design by downloading and testing it as in the "Quick Start OR-Gate lab."

Downloading and Testing Your Design

Step 7:
Download the design to the board as in the "Quick Start OR-Gate lab."

Step 8:
To test the design, use the switches on the board and observe the LEDs. Refer to your lab book to verify which pins are connected to the switches and LEDs.

Step 9:
Give a brief explanation of the difference between the cout and overflow outputs.

_____

_____

_____

_____

Step 10:
Give a brief explanation of how the 8-bit adder/subtractor circuit works.

_____

_____

_____

_____

Experiment 58 1-of-8 Decoder Lab

Introduction

The purpose of this lab is to build, simulate, and download a 1-of-8 ROM address decoder circuit using the Xilinx Foundation tools and Digilab Spartan board.

Objectives

After completing this lab, students will be able to:
- Demonstrate the operation of the circuit described.
- Perform a simple functional and timing simulation using the integrated simulation tool.

Preliminary Procedure

Follow the same steps as in the "Quick Start OR-Gate lab" to set up the lab board.

Procedure

Create a new design with the Xilinx Foundation Series Schematic and name the design ROMDEC. You want to create a design that looks like Figure 1:

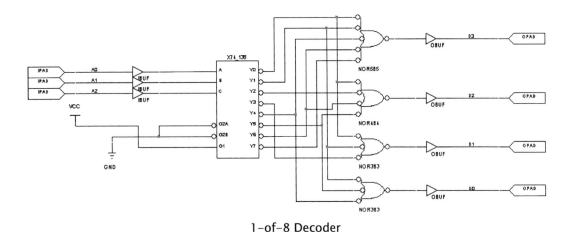

1-of-8 Decoder

Figure 1

1) Once you finish creating the desired schematic, make sure to save it. <u>Click</u> **File → Save**. Ensure that you have locked pins according to the board you are using. See the appendix for common board pinouts.

2) Return to the Foundation Project Manager (press **<Alt>** + **<Tab>** to task switch).

3) The design entry is finished.

4) Next you need to implement the design the same way as in the Quick Start OR-Gate lab.

5) Click on the Implementation icon in the Project Manager window and follow the same procedure as in previous labs.

Activity Sheet Experiment 58
1-of-8 Decoder Lab

Name: _____

Date: _____

Using the Simulator

Step 1:
To simulate the operation of the circuits, first click on the SIM icon in the menu bar at the top of the schematic screen. The Logic Simulator will open.

Step 2:
Next, click on Signal -> Add Signals in the menu bar at the top of the simulator screen. Here you can decide which signals to drive and observe during the simulation. Note that the signals available are A0-A2, as well as the outputs: D0-D3 (from the schematic), and SimGlobalReset. Recall that what SimGlobalReset does is to simulate a global reset on the PLD. It is always a good idea to use this initially just to ensure that you have a totally reset simulation before you start to drive signals.
Double-click on all of the signals (there will be a red checkmark to indicate selection). Then click on CLOSE at the bottom of the screen.

Step 3:
Now click on Signals -> Add Stimulators in the menu bar at the top of the simulator screen. A box that looks like a keyboard will open. Click on the signal "A0" in the upper-left portion of the screen and then on the "Q" on the keyboard (on the screen). Do the same for "A1" using the "W" key on the keyboard. Continue in this manner until you are driving all of the inputs.

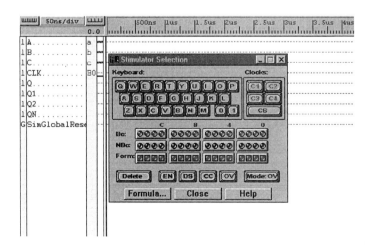

Step 4:
Toggle the "R" and the "A0-A2" signals, then click on the "footsteps" in the menu bar at the top of the screen. Verify that the outputs follow the truth tables in the text.

Step 5:
You can perform a timing simulation of this same design by simply changing the pull-down menu in the menu bar from "Functional" to "Timing". Now you can physically verify this design by downloading and testing it as in the "Quick Start OR-Gate lab."

Downloading and Testing Your Design

Step 6:
Download the design to the board as in the "Quick Start OR-Gate lab."

Step 7:
To test the design, use the switches on the board and observe the LEDs. Refer to your lab book to verify which pins are connected to the switches and LEDs.

Step 8:
Give a brief explanation of how the 1-of-8 decoder circuit works.

_____

_____

_____

_____

Experiment 59 64-X-8 RAM Lab

Introduction

The purpose of this lab is to build, simulate, and download a 64-X-8 RAM circuit using the Xilinx Foundation tools and Digilab Spartan board.

Objectives

After completing this lab, students will be able to:
- Demonstrate the operation of the RAM described.
- Perform a simple functional and timing simulation using the integrated simulation tool.

Preliminary Procedure

Follow the same steps as in the "Quick Start OR-Gate lab" to set up the lab board.

Procedure

Create a new design with the Xilinx Foundation Series Schematic and name the design ADDSUB. You want to create a design that looks like Figure 1:

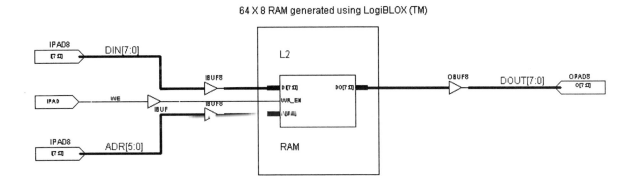

64-X-8 RAM

Figure 1

1) Once you finish creating the desired schematic, make sure to save it. <u>Click</u> **File → Save**. Ensure that you have locked pins according to the board you are using. See the appendix for common board pinouts.

2) Then return to the Foundation Project Manager (press **<Alt>** + **<Tab>** to task switch). Note: Be sure to name the busses as in previous labs where bussing was used or the circuit will not simulate properly.

3) The design entry is finished.

4) Next you need to implement the design the same way as in the Quick Start OR-Gate lab.

5) Click on the Implementation icon in the Project Manager window and follow the same procedure as in previous labs.

Activity Sheet Experiment 59
64-X-8 RAM Lab

Name: _____

Date: _____

Using the Simulator

Step 1:
To simulate the operation of the RAM, first click on the SIM icon in the menu bar at the top of the schematic screen. The Logic Simulator will open.

Step 2:
Next, click on Signal -> Add Signals in the menu bar at the top of the simulator screen. Here you can decide which signals to drive and observe during the simulation. Note that the signals available are ADR[7:0],WE, and DIN[7:0], as well as the outputs: DOUT[7:0] (from the schematic), and something called SimGlobalReset. Recall that what SimGlobalReset does is to simulate a global reset on the PLD. It is always a good idea to use this initially just to ensure that you have a totally reset simulation before you start to drive signals.
Double-click on all of the signals (there will be a red checkmark to indicate selection). Then click on CLOSE at the bottom of the screen.

Step 3:
Select the bus signal ADR[7:0] and right-click. Then select Bus>Flatten to expand the bus to individual signals ADR0, ADR1, ADR2, etc. Do the same for the DIN bus.

Step 4:
Now click on Signals -> Add Stimulators in the menu bar at the top of the simulator screen. A box that looks like a keyboard will open. Click on the signal "ADR0" in the upper-left portion of the screen and then on the "A" on the keyboard (on the screen). Do the same for ADR1 using the letter "S" and with ADR2-5, DIN0-7, and WE using other letters on the keyboard screen. Then click on "SimGlobalReset" and then on the keyboard click on "R". We can now drive the inputs and the global reset. Pressing the "R" key will toggle the reset and pressing the "A" key will toggle the "ADR0" input to the adder, and so on.

Step 5:
Toggle the "R" and the input signals and then click on the "footsteps" in the menu bar at the top of the screen. Verify that the circuit works using the truth table provided in the text.

Step 6:
You can perform a timing simulation of this same design by simply changing the pull-down menu in the menu bar from "Functional" to "Timing".

Now you can physically verify this design by downloading and testing it as in the "Quick Start OR-Gate lab."

Downloading and Testing Your Design

Step 7:
Download the design to the Digilab Spartan board as in the "Quick Start OR-Gate lab."

Step 8:
To test the design, use the switches on the board and observe the LEDs. Refer to your lab book to verify which pins are connected to the switches and LEDs.

Step 9:
Give a brief explanation of why you can implement RAM in an FPGA and not in a CPLD.

_____

_____

_____

_____

Step 10:
Give a brief explanation of how the 64-X-8 RAM circuit works.

_____

_____

_____

_____

APPENDIX

Using Hardware Design Languages (HDLs)
with Xilinx tools

This tutorial is not meant to teach you either VHDL or Verilog. The purpose of this brief tutorial is to get you familiar with how these languages look so that you will know something about them when you inevitably run into them in your career or take a class in one of these languages.

VHDL and Verilog are the two major hardware design languages in use in industry today. Another HDL language, ABEL, is an older tool that is no longer being used as much as it once was. VHDL was created under the auspices of the United States government for use in military designs. A design automation company called Cadence created Verilog. For our purposes the two languages perform the same function and differ only in their format.

A hardware design language is a method of describing digital logic using a high-level language (text) instead of a schematic drawing. This method is preferred for large designs because each function can be broken out into a single file and debugged before it is integrated into the rest of the design. This general design method is known as hierarchical design. The Xilinx tools allow a designer to use schematics, VHDL, ABEL, and Verilog all in the same design, using hierarchical methods.

We are going to start by creating a decoder using VHDL and then do the same thing in Verilog.

1) First open the Program Manager and create a new project called "decoder" using the same method as described in the "Quick Start OR-Gate" lab.

2) Select "HDL" in the New Project window and then OK.

3) Next, click on the HDL Editor icon in the Design Entry block and select Use HDL Design Wizard. Click on Next and select VHDL (we will do Verilog next and the only difference will be the code you type and the selection made in this window). You are

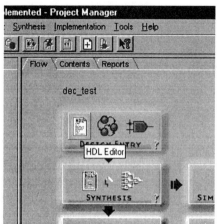

going to create the same input and output ports as you did in the schematic version of this lab: inputs A, B, C, AA, and BB, and outputs Y, Output1, Output2, Output3, and Output4.

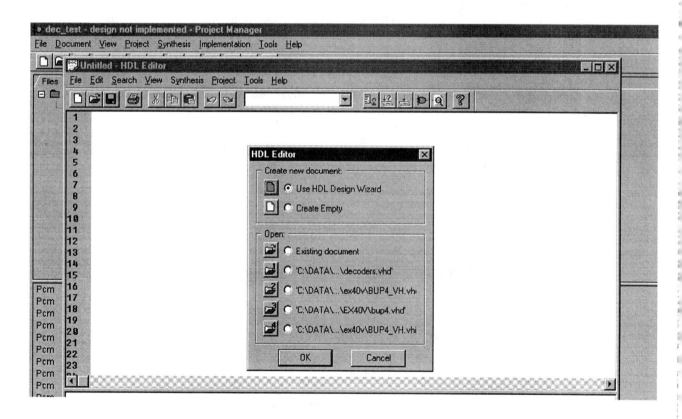

4) Click on Next and New to add the inputs and outputs to the design.

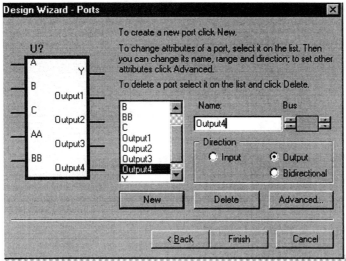

5) Click on Finish when you have added the ports. A window will open that has the basic declarations for the ports that you created. Now you need to add the architectural statements that will actually perform the decoding function.

```
decoder - HDL Editor
File  Edit  Search  View  Synthesis  Project  Tools  Help

1   library IEEE;
2   use IEEE.std_logic_1164.all;
3
4   entity decoder is
5       port (
6           A: in STD_LOGIC;
7           B: in STD_LOGIC;
8           C: in STD_LOGIC;
9           AA: in STD_LOGIC;
10          BB: in STD_LOGIC;
11          Y: out STD_LOGIC;
12          Output1: out STD_LOGIC;
13          Output2: out STD_LOGIC;
14          Output3: out STD_LOGIC;
15          Output4: out STD_LOGIC
16      );
17  end decoder;
18
19  architecture decoder_arch of decoder is
20  begin
21      -- <<enter your statements here>>
22  end decoder_arch;
23
```

6) Enter the following lines in between begin and end to complete the design:

$$Y <= (A \text{ and } (\text{not } B) \text{ and } (\text{not } C));$$
$$OUTPUT1 <= (\text{not } AA) \text{ and } (\text{not } BB);$$
$$OUTPUT2 <= (\text{not } AA) \text{ and } BB;$$
$$OUTPUT3 <= AA \text{ and } (\text{not } BB);$$
$$OUTPUT4 <= AA \text{ and } BB;$$

7) Here is what the complete file looks like along with comments that explain what the code is doing.
8) Next, click on the Synthesis pull-down menu and select Synthesize. Assuming you did

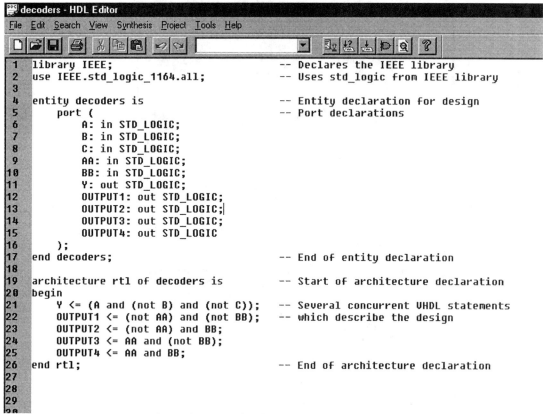

```
library IEEE;                              -- Declares the IEEE library
use IEEE.std_logic_1164.all;               -- Uses std_logic from IEEE library

entity decoders is                         -- Entity declaration for design
    port (                                 -- Port declarations
        A: in STD_LOGIC;
        B: in STD_LOGIC;
        C: in STD_LOGIC;
        AA: in STD_LOGIC;
        BB: in STD_LOGIC;
        Y: out STD_LOGIC;
        OUTPUT1: out STD_LOGIC;
        OUTPUT2: out STD_LOGIC;
        OUTPUT3: out STD_LOGIC;
        OUTPUT4: out STD_LOGIC
    );
end decoders;                              -- End of entity declaration

architecture rtl of decoders is            -- Start of architecture declaration
begin
    Y <= (A and (not B) and (not C));      -- Several concurrent VHDL statements
    OUTPUT1 <= (not AA) and (not BB);      -- which describe the design
    OUTPUT2 <= (not AA) and BB;
    OUTPUT3 <= AA and (not BB);
    OUTPUT4 <= AA and BB;
end rtl;                                   -- End of architecture declaration
```

not have any errors, you have just synthesized your first VHDL design!
9) Now go back to the Project Manager window and select Add Source Files from the Synthesis pull-down menu and add your file decoder. You need to synthesize the design once again, specifically for the Xilinx device you are using such as the SPARTAN XCS10.
10) Next, click on the "decoders.ucf" file. This file allows you to lock the signals to specific pins so that you will be able to download the design to a specific board (in this case the Digilab Spartan board) and test the design.
11) Now you are ready to implement and download the design the same way as described in the "Quick Start OR-Gate" lab.

12) Now we will do the same design using the Verilog language.
Follow the same steps as above with the exception of selecting Verilog in the design wizard
and using the code:

```
decoders - HDL Editor
File  Edit  Search  View  Synthesis  Project  Tools  Help

1    module decoders (A, B, C, AA, BB, Y, OUTPUT1, OUTPUT2, OUTPUT3, OUTPUT4);
2        input A;
3        input B;
4        input C;
5        input AA;
6        input BB;
7        output Y;
8        output OUTPUT1;
9        output OUTPUT2;
10       output OUTPUT3;
11       output OUTPUT4;
12
13       reg Y;
14       reg OUTPUT1;
15       reg OUTPUT2;
16       reg OUTPUT3;
17       reg OUTPUT4;
18
19       always @(A or B or C or AA or BB)
20           begin: decode
21               Y = (A & ~B & ~C);
22               OUTPUT1 = ~AA & ~BB;
23               OUTPUT2 = ~AA & BB;
24               OUTPUT3 = AA & ~BB;
25               OUTPUT4 = AA & BB;
26           end
27   endmodule
28
29
30
31
```

Hint: If you used the design wizard, you will only have to enter the part starting with "reg y"
since the design wizard will put the input and output declarations in the design for you.

Now follow steps 8 through 11 as above and you will have done a Verilog implementation of
the decoder design. We will continue to show you VHDL and Verilog versions of these
designs in selected labs for the rest of the text where appropriate.

A Brief Tutorial on "Locking" Pins and Configuring an FPGA
(Courtesy of Clint Cole, Digilab, Inc.)

Configuring the FPGA with a circuit

All signals on the Digilab board that connect the buttons, switches, and LEDs to the J2 connector are connected to the Xilinx FPGA chip as well (a table showing the FPGA pinout is available on page 29 of the Digilab users manual at the www.digilent.cc website). Any circuit implemented in the FPGA can use the buttons and switches as inputs and the LEDs as outputs. To connect an FPGA-based circuit to these devices, you must include information in your schematic to "map" circuit inputs and outputs to particular FPGA pins. Mapping is accomplished by including special components in your schematic called IPADs, IBUFs, OPADs, and OBUFs. These components exist solely to allow you to define physical pin connections, and so they only need be used in circuit schematics that you intend to download.

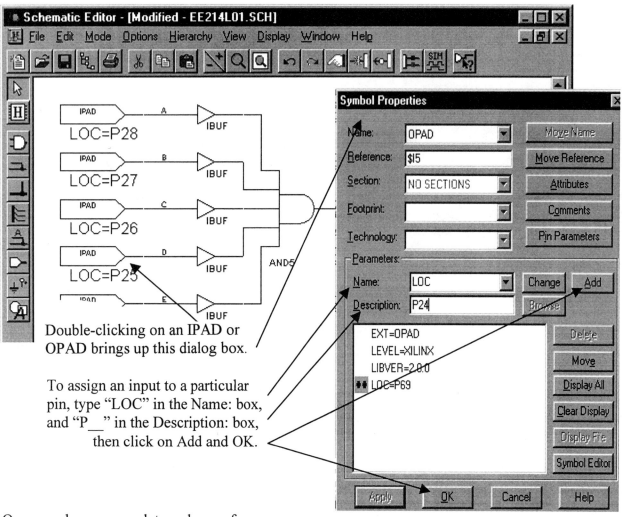

Once you have a complete and error-free schematic, you may add IBUFs and IPADs to all inputs, and OBUFs and OPADs to all outputs. Then, the IPADs and OPADs can be connected to particular pins by double-clicking the pads and entering the "LOC" parameter and pin number in the appropriate fields (Name and Description, respectively).

310

In the example circuit above, switch inputs on the Digilab board have been connected to the circuit inputs. Note that the input names (A, B, C, D, etc.) have been added to the wires between the IPADs and IBUFs – this allows the simulator to find the nets using the assigned signal names. If this circuit were downloaded to the FPGA, then SW1 would drive input A, SW2 would drive input B, and so on.

Once all IPADs, IBUFs, OPADs, and OBUFs have been added and edited with pin locations, you can begin the implementation process by choosing the "Implementation" button from the Xilinx main screen. In the first dialog box that appears, choose Yes to update the netlist from the schematic editor. In the second dialog box, make sure the device is S10PC84 and speed is 3 before proceeding; the version and revision names can use the defaults. Press the Run button, and then wait for the status window showing Translate, Map, Place & Route, Timing, and Configure processes to terminate. Before proceeding further, make sure that the Digilab board is powered on and connected to the PC via the parallel cable, and that SW9 is in the PROG position. Then select the Programming option from the Xilinx main window, and "hardware debugger" from the subsequent dialog box. The cable should be auto-detected; if not, manually choose the parallel cable in the Cable → communications dialog box. Once the cable has been detected, you can download your design simply by double-clicking on the appropriate file name in the hardware debugger window.

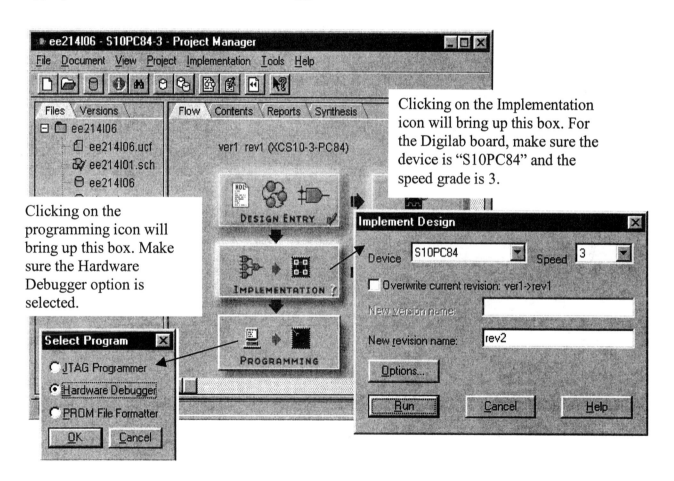

Clicking on the Implementation icon will bring up this box. For the Digilab board, make sure the device is "S10PC84" and the speed grade is 3.

Clicking on the programming icon will bring up this box. Make sure the Hardware Debugger option is selected.

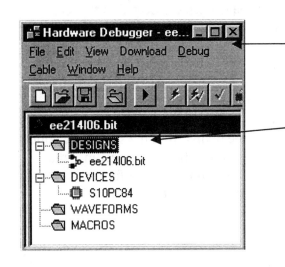

This window will be displayed after selecting the Hardware Debugger Programming option.

Double-click *filename.bit* to cause the file to be downloaded. In this case, a Xilinx design project named ee214l06 will be downloaded.

After completing this process, the circuit that you designed will be resident in the FPGA device and ready for use.

Pin Tables for Digilab Spartan, Spartan XL, and XESS, XS40, and XS95 Boards.

For latest information see www.digilab.cc**,** www.xess.com **,** xup.msu.edu **or** www.university.xilinx.com

Digilab XL (new) Spartan Pinout

Pin #	Function	Pin #	Function	Pin #	Function
1	GND	29	O1	57	BTN3
2	Vdd	30	M1_NC	58	BTN2
3	PWE	31	GND	59	BTN1
4	PD0	32	MODE	60	LD8
5	PD1	33	Vdd	61	LD7
6	PD2	34	M2_NC	62	LD6
7	PD3	35	CLK2	63	Vdd
8	PD4	36	O2	64	GND
9	PAS	37	O3	65	LD5
10	PRS	38	A4	66	LD4
11	Vdd	39	A3	67	LD3
12	GND	40	A2	68	LD2
13	CLK1	41	INIT (O4)	69	LD1
14	PDS	42	Vdd	70	LDG
15	PWT	43	GND	71	DIN (O5)
16	PD5	44	A1	72	DOUT(RXD)
17	PD7	45	CG	73	CCLK
18	PD6	46	CF	74	Vdd
19	SW8	47	CE	75	TXD(PINT)
20	SW7	48	CD	76	GND
21	GND	49	CC	77	R
22	Vdd	50	CB	78	G
23	SW6	51	CA	79	B
24	SW5	52	GND	80	HS
25	SW4	53	DONE	81	VS
26	SW3	54	Vdd	82	PS2C
27	SW2	55	PROG	83	PS2D
28	SW1	56	BTN4	84	PINT

Digilab (original) Spartan Pinout

Pin #	Function	Pin #	Function	Pin #	Function
1	GND	29	CG	57	CLK2
2	Vdd	30	M1_NC	58	BTN2
3	PWE	31	GND	59	BTN1
4	PD0	32	MODE	60	LD8
5	PD1	33	Vdd	61	LD7
6	PD2	34	M2_NC	62	LD6
7	PD3	35	CF	63	Vdd
8	PD4	36	CE	64	GND
9	PAS	37	CD	65	LD5
10	PRS	38	CC	66	LD4
11	Vdd	39	CB	67	LD3
12	GND	40	CA	68	LD2
13	CLK1	41	INIT (O4)	69	LD1
14	PDS	42	Vdd	70	LDG
15	PWT	43	GND	71	DIN (O5)
16	PD5	44	O1	72	DOUT(RXD)
17	PD7	45	O2	73	CCLK
18	PD6	46	O3	74	Vdd
19	SW8	47	A4	75	TDO(PINT)
20	SW7	48	A3	76	GND
21	GND	49	A2	77	TXD
22	Vdd	50	A1	78	R
23	SW6	51	BTN4	79	G
24	SW5	52	GND	80	B
25	SW4	53	DONE	81	VS
26	SW3	54	Vdd	82	HS
27	SW2	55	PROG	83	PS2C
28	SW1	56	BTN3	84	PS2D

XS40 & XSTEND Board Pin Mapping

(DIPSW* and D_* mappings shown below are correct for pre-production XSTENDboards v1.0, used in workshops. Their orders will be reversed in production boards.)

XS40 Bus (J1,J3,J18)	XS95 Pins (J2)	Power/ GND	DIP Switch	Push-buttons	LEDs	VGA Interface	PS/2 Interface	RAMs	Stereo Codec	8051 Uc	PC Parallel Port	Oscillator	Function	UW-FPGABOARD Pin
1	77												Uncommitted XS95 I/O pin	
2	78	+5V											+5V power source	
3	1				LS_0			A0					LED segment; address line	P35
4	2				LS_1			A1					LED segment; address line	P36
5	3				LS_2			A2					LED segment; address line	P29
6	5		DIPSW4						LRCK	P13			DIP switch; codec control; uC I/O	P24
7	6		DIPSW1					LCE_		P10			DIP switch; RAM chip-enable, uC I/O port	P19
8	7		DIPSW2					RCE_		P11			DIP switch; RAM chip-enable, uC I/O port	P20
9	11		DIPSW3						MCLK	P12			DIP switch; codec clock; uC I/O port	P23
10	35				D_8			AD7		P07			LED; RAM data line; uC muxed address/data line	P61
11	31												Uncommitted XS95 I/O pin	
12	69												Uncommitted XS95 I/O pin	
13	9											CLK	XS40/95 oscillator output	
14	13									PSEN_			uC program storage-enable	
15	28												JTAG TDI; DIN	
16	30												JTAG TCK; CCLK	
17	29												JTAG TMS	
18	14			S5		RED1							XS Board LED segment; VGA color signal	
19	15			S6		HSYNC_							XS Board LED segment; VGA horiz. sync.	
20	17			S3		GREEN1							XS Board LED segment; VGA color signal	
21	68												Uncommitted XS95 I/O pin	
22	33												Uncommitted XS95 I/O pin	
23	18			S4		RED0							XS Board LED segment; VGA color signal	
24	19			S2		GREEN0							XS Board LED segment; VGA color signal	
25	21			S0		BLUE0							XS Board LED segment; VGA color signal	
26	23			S1		BLUE1							XS Board LED segment; VGA color signal	
27	32									RD_			uC read line	
28	34			RDP_				A15		P27			LED decimal-point; address line; uC I/O port	P41
29	20									ALE_			uC address-latch-enable	
30													Serial EEPROM chip-enable	
31	12												Uncommitted XS95 I/O pin	
32	81										PC_D6		PC parallel port output	
33	25												Uncommitted XS95 I/O pin	
34	80										PC_D7		PC parallel port output	
35	39				D_5			AD4		P04			LED; RAM data line; uC muxed address/data line	P66
36	45									RST			uC reset line	
37	10			RESET_						XTAL1			Pushbutton; uC clock line	P56
38	40				D_4			AD3		P03			LED; RAM data line; uC muxed address/data line	P57
39	41				D_3			AD2		P02			LED; RAM data line; uC muxed address/data line	P58
40	43				D_2			AD1		P01			LED; RAM data line; uC muxed address/data line	P59
41	44				D_1			AD0		P00			LED; RAM data line; uC muxed address/data line	P60
42	4												Uncommitted XS95 I/O pin	
43													Unconnected	
44	46								CCLK		PC_D0		Codec control line; PC parallel port output	
45	47								CDIN		PC_D1		Codec control line; PC parallel port output	
46	48								CS_		PC_D2		Codec control line; PC parallel port output	
47	50										PC_D3		PC parallel port output	
48	51										PC_D4		PC parallel port output	
49	52										PC_D5		PC parallel port output	
50	53				RS_4			A12		P24			LED segment; address line; uC I/O port	P48
51	54				RS_2			A10		P22			LED segment; address line; uC I/O port	P45
52	49	GND											Power supply ground	
53													Unconnected	
54		+3.3V											+3.3V/+5V power supply (4000E/4000XL)	
55			PROGRAM										XS40 configuration control	P55
56	55				RS_3			A11		P23			LED segment; address line; uC I/O port	P51
57	56				RS_1			A9		P21			LED segment; address line; uC I/O port	P47
58	57				RS_5			A13		P25			LED segment; address line; uC I/O port	P50
59	58				RS_0			A8		P20			LED segment; address line; uC I/O port	P46
60	61				RS_6			A14		P26			LED segment; address line; uC I/O port	P43
61	62							OE_					RAM output-enable	
62	63							WR_		P36			RAM write-enable; uC I/O port	
63													Unconnected	
64													Unconnected	
65	65							CE_					XS Board RAM chip-enable	
66	66		DIPSW7						SDOUT	P16			DIP switch; codec output data; uC I/O port	P27
67	24,67			SPARE_		VSYNC_				P17			Pushbutton; VGA vert. sync.; uC I/O port	P18
68	26						KB_CLK			P34			PS/2 keyboard clock; uC I/O port	
69	70		DIPSW8				KB_DATA			P31			DIP switch; keyboard serial data; uC I/O port	P28
70	71		DIPSW6						SDIN	P15			DIP switch; codec input data; uC I/O port	P26
71	28												JTAG TDI; DIN	
72	59												JTAG TDO; DOUT	
73	30												JTAG TCK; CCLK	
74	74												Uncommitted XS95 I/O pin	
75	59												JTAG TDO; DOUT	
76	76												Uncommitted XS95 I/O pin	
77	72		DIPSW5						SCLK	P14			DIP switch; codec serial clock; uC I/O port	P25
78	75				LS_3			A3					LED segment; address line	P44
79	79				LS_4			A4					LED segment; address line	P38
80	36				D_7			AD6		P06			LED; RAM data line; uC muxed address/data line	P62
81	37				D_6			AD5		P05			LED; RAM data line; uC muxed address/data line	P65
82	82				LS_5			A5					LED segment; address line	P40
83	83				LS_6			A6					LED segment; address line	P39
84	84				LDP_			A7					LED decimal-point; address line	P37